# Producing and Consuming the Craft Beer Movement

*Producing and Consuming the Craft Beer Movement* is an ethnographic analysis of the craft beer movement and its rapid development as an industry that articulated a different set of values: celebrating, quality, community, and good taste.

This book will provide an excellent foundation for considering craft beer and an entrepreneurial practice that produces other forms of value beyond monetary value. The craft beer movement has been an important movement for thinking about contemporary consumer culture, and how that consumer culture might develop a very different set of values and priorities from those of the dominant consumer culture that is created by large-scale industries focused on the instrumental values of profit and efficiency. Located in one site, the ethnography is situated within the larger context of the rise of digital media, the evolution of cities, and the latest stage of the capitalist marketplace. The book is distinctive as it is ethnographic in its methodology. It is focused on one locale, the metropolitan area around Philadelphia. Philadelphia, along with Boston, Denver, San Diego, and a few other cities, was a central location for the early development of the craft beer industry. With its interdisciplinary approach, individuals with interests in digital and social media, consumer culture, political economy, ethnography, and contemporary cultural theory will find this an interesting case study of an important industry that developed from the homebrewing movement to become an important craft industry that is now a global phenomenon.

This book is directed to a broad range of readers interested in new media, consumer culture, craft, and contemporary capitalist culture. The book embeds the local in the larger historical and political economic context. Readers would include faculty members in communication, media studies, cultural studies, sociology, and anthropology. Students at a graduate and upper level undergraduate level would be interested as well.

**Wesley Shumar** is a Professor in the Department of Communication at Drexel University. His research is focused on the commodification of culture, the cultural production of value, the transformation of space, time, and communicative interaction through digital technologies, and the social and interactive processes of learning. His work on higher education focuses on the cultural and spatial transformation of American universities within an increasingly consumerist economy. His work on learning focuses on the ways the internet and digital technologies can enhance learning interactions. He is currently exploring the craft economy and the production of value. He is the author of *College for Sale: A Critique of the Commodification of Higher Education* and *Inside Mathforum.org: Analysis of an Online Mathematics Education Community*. He is also the co-editor of *Structure and Agency in the Neoliberal University* and *Building Virtual Communities: Learning and Change in Cyberspace*.

**Tyson Mitman** is a senior lecturer in Sociology and Criminology at York St John University. His research examines space and culture. Specifically, how culture and space intersect and interact with each other, how we make our lives through the cultural groups and practices we value, and how we position and debate power, identity, and representation through how we construct differing cultural groups and how those groups are differently allowed to use public and private spaces. Much of his research has been about public aesthetics and graffiti culture. It has focused on how individuals who write graffiti construct their identity within their subculture, how their interaction with public space produces a type of political discourse, and how graffiti affects spaces and those who use those spaces. He is the author of *The Art of Defiance: Graffiti, Politics, and the Reimagined City in Philadelphia*. He cares deeply about craft beer and respects the producers who are driven by a desire to produce the best product they can, not merely the most profitable one. He believes, at its best, craft beer (and most craft production) helps make caring and informed communities who are capable of resisting the corporate mediocrity mass production so often tries to heap onto all of us.

**Routledge Critical Beverage Studies**
Series edited by Peter J. Howland, Jennifer Smith Maguire and Catherine May Tucker

***Routledge Critical Beverage Studies*** offers cutting edge and ground-breaking insights on beverages as vehicles for a wide array of social, cultural, economic, environment and political phenomenon. Books in the series are interdisciplinary and multi-methodological, exploring a variety of perspectives from the social sciences and humanities.

**The Wine & The Gift**
From Production to Consumption
*Edited by Peter J. Howland*

**Producing and Consuming the Craft Beer Movement**
*Wesley Shumar and Tyson Mitman*

For more information about this series, please visit: https://www.routledge.com/Routledge-Critical-Beverage-Studies/book-series/CBS

# Producing and Consuming the Craft Beer Movement

Wesley Shumar and Tyson Mitman

Routledge
Taylor & Francis Group
LONDON AND NEW YORK

First published 2023
by Routledge
4 Park Square, Milton Park, Abingdon, Oxon OX14 4RN

and by Routledge
605 Third Avenue, New York, NY 10158

*Routledge is an imprint of the Taylor & Francis Group, an informa business*



*British Library Cataloguing-in-Publication Data*
A catalogue record for this book is available from the British Library

ISBN: 978-0-367-62559-7 (hbk)
ISBN: 978-0-367-62560-3 (pbk)
ISBN: 978-1-003-10968-6 (ebk)

DOI: 10.4324/9781003109686

Typeset in Times New Roman
by KnowledgeWorks Global Ltd.

# Contents

# Figures

# Acknowledgments

When we began this project, we were three. It was at the beginning a side project for all of us. It was very central to our theoretical concerns, but we were all engaged in other projects as we began this work. Over time, Nora Madison, because of other work commitments felt, could not continue with the project and so she is not listed as a co-author by her choice. But we feel Nora's presence throughout this work. She was with us as we conceived of the project, she learned to brew beer with us and brought her network of brewing connections to help us along the way. She participated in interviewing brewers and went to beer events with us. We owe a great deal to Nora Madison and her insights into contemporary culture, digital and social media, and specifically her insights into craft beer culture. This book is better because of her participation. Of course, all the errors are ours alone, and we only wish Nora had been able to continue to correct more of our errors. We also thank Nick Coffman, who joined the project as we were finishing up chapters to help edit the final draft. Nick's careful attention to detail has been invaluable. And further, Nick's interest in the craft beer scene contributed to many late-stage decisions. We had some wonderful discussions and learned a lot from Nick's experiences in the craft beer industry. Thanks to Carol Brandt for the many conversations about the status of craft beer, the visits to breweries and events, and the tastings and reviewing of craft beers. Thanks to Paige Davis, Fisher, and West Mitman for enduring Tyson during the researching and writing of this book, and just generally. Thanks to Eric Hartline, and Brew Your Own Beer, for the entrée into the craft beer community and for his guidance in brewing and the support provided to the local homebrewing community. Many thanks to the brewers, owners, marketing and salespeople, and educators in the industry who participated in formal and informal interviews and who allowed us to watch what they do. They provided tremendous insight into this fascinating and ever-changing industry and culture. We would be remiss if we did not also thank all of the craft brewers out there dedicating their time, energy, and creativity to producing great beer. Thank you for what you do. This goes for the dedicated home brewers all the way up through the craft brewery brewing thousands and thousands of barrels a year. Your commitment to your craft, your efforts to expand what beer can be while also maintaining what it always has been, and all your efforts to build an informed and committed community around craft beer matter. Your work is valuable, and we genuinely appreciate that you do it. We would also like to extend our respect to all of those brewers who have resisted the siren song of a hefty corporate buyout and to all those who will. Your commitment to your values is one of the major reasons the craft beer community is as strong and devoted as it is.

We thank and acknowledge the following for allowing us to reprint: Aviva Kaminsky for the use of her photo of Fiume Bar; special thanks to the Brewers Association for artwork used on pages 6, 9, 27 and 40. This artwork includes Brewers Association Independent Craft Brewer Seal, Recent U.S. Brewery Count, Historical Craft Brewery Production by Category, and U.S. Craft Brewery by Category.

# 1 Introduction

## The Craft Community

### Introduction

We began this project as a professor and two graduate students in Philadelphia. Wesley Shumar is a cultural anthropologist whose research has focused on the commodification of culture and the use of digital media and the internet in education. Tyson Mitman was a doctoral student in the program whose dissertation work looked at the graffiti community in Philadelphia and the evolution of graffiti in Philadelphia. Nora Madison was a doctoral student studying the bisexual community online and the ways that community was working to make themselves seen among the LGBTQ+ community. All three of us were in the graduate program in Communication, Culture, and Media at Drexel University. The project began when Madison and Mitman were still graduate students. They are now faculty at different institutions, Mitman is at a university in the UK and Madison is at a College in Philadelphia. When Madison graduated, she had other research and publication commitments. Shumar and Mitman continued with the craft beer project and are the authors of this book. Although Madison left the project, her contribution was very significant. She participated in a number of the interviews. She became a brewer along with us as we transitioned into participant observers. She participated in Philly Beer Week and other craft beer events. She was a co-author on early conference papers. Her ideas have helped to shape our thinking and while she did not see herself as an author of this text, her voice is interwoven throughout our chapters.

Any research project begins before it begins. And our beginnings grew out of a set of experiences we began to have in relationship to craft beer. It began to form our relationship to the subject matter before we were conscious of the fact that a relationship and a set of concerns were beginning to develop. Here we tell two stories that inform this sense of a beginning before the beginning. Along with the University of Pennsylvania, Drexel University is situated in a part of West Philadelphia called University City. As the contemporary hipster movement began to gain traction among university students and other young adults in the area, there was the same kind of resistance to mainstream society and consumer capitalism that one found in earlier hipster

DOI: 10.4324/9781003109686-1

and hippie movements. However, the current movement was both ironic about its own position as it attempted to create an alternative economy in the West Philadelphia neighborhood. There were crust punk cafes, alternative food co-ops, and other consumer establishments. One such establishment was Fiume bar, (see Figure 1.1) a small bar above an Ethiopian restaurant called Abyssinia. Fiume was a small, overcrowded bar, a few mismatched stools, some of which were in bad repair. It was not a comfortable place to be and its "hipness" was perhaps located in the very discomfort around "upmarket" consumption.

One evening after a late Friday afternoon colloquium, we randomly walked into the restaurant and went up the steps to check out the bar. Shumar, whose interest in craft beer had been growing, immediately noticed that there was a nice selection of "hip" craft beers in bottles. The bar was so small and impromptu that there were no taps. And craft beer, while not new, was not yet a widespread phenomenon, especially if you were chasing after some of the more prestigious beers that did not yet have a wide general audience. Mitman started ordering "city wides," a shot of whisky and a Pabst Blue Ribbon (PBR) beer. Pabst, interestingly, has had a reputation for being a "hip" beer across several generations, although it is really just another adjunct lager and really does not stand out from beers like Miller and Budweiser. But perhaps their smaller market and reputation is what made it hip.[1] While Shumar was aware that PBR was hip and went through his own youth drinking PBR, he playfully said to Mitman, "hey, you can't drink that stuff when there is good beer here." Mitman replied that he drank the PBR because it was cheap, and not just because it was cool. And it was cheap at $3 a bottle. So, Shumar bought Mitman a Bell's Two Hearted Ale.

Bell's Two Hearted Ale, first hit the market in 1997. It has often been called one of the America's best IPAs. It currently has a score of 95 on Beer Advocate, a prominent craft beer website and former craft beer magazine, which makes it "world class" by their designation. At this writing, there are 15,667 ratings of Two Hearted, which is a lot of ratings for such a high score. Larry Bell opened Bell's Brewery in 1985, making it one of the early craft breweries in America. While Two Hearted began in 1997, it became a year around release in 2003 and in 2013 it became their best-selling beer. In the 2003–2013 period, Bell's expanded its brewery operation and got more beer into more states. So, in 2012, when we were in Fiume bar in West Philadelphia, Two Hearted was beginning to be available, but it also was seen as a very special beer when you ran across it.

In that moment, Mitman's opinion of beer changed forever. As a young grad student with little money, Mitman saw beer as a way to chase whisky and a way to relax. He did not see it as anything more than that. After drinking the Two Hearted, a whole world of taste exploration was opened up for him. He no longer saw beer as an inexpensive chemically induced relaxation technique. Beer was now an aesthetic experience, something to be savored and contemplated. Funnily, Mitman did not tell Shumar about this realization at the time. It would be several years later before he told the story. But along with Madison, the three of them began to explore beers.

*Figure 1.1* Fiume Bar Photo

Source: Photo by Aviva Kaminsky.

The second story begins in 30th street train station, a large, beautiful train station in West Philadelphia. For two terms in early 2012, Shumar was teaching classes in the evening. After his class, he went to the train station and would order a beer in the bar in the train station and look up reviews in Beer Advocate and attempt to taste the things in the beer that other reviewers tasted. By this point, Mitman, Madison, and Shumar were very interested in the growing craft beer movement. They not only enjoyed going to bars and checking out beers, but as members of the Communication, Culture and Media program, they were interested in consumer culture and the craft scene as a growing phenomenon. 2008 was the first Philly Beer Week and by 2012 it had become a very major event, its first night really taking over the whole city. So, we began to see craft beer as a social movement and one that was very interesting.

As Shumar continued this practice of ordering a beer, tasting it, and evaluating it according to other people's reviews and the tasting guideline that the Beer Advocate website had set up, he began to realize that this was a very large online community and one that was focused on a particular kind of education of the palate, much like one finds in the wine community. The three of us then began this process on a regular basis. When we had a beer together, it was not just an end of the day ritual, it was an immersion into the informal education of our collective palate. Over time, we would come to see this online community as much more than a repository of reviews of good beers. The internet, and the digital tools linked to the internet, became the place where brewers shared recipes, shared brewing problems, and discussed solutions. It was the way to connect to used equipment that you might need for your brewing operation. Later, through social media, the internet became one of the ways to market your product and your brewery. And it became the place where consumers became co-producers as they helped market and evaluate beers and breweries. And so, with our interest in consumer culture and digital media, craft beer started to seem like a logical area of study for us, even if it began as a side project for all three of us.

## What Is Craft?

Studying craft beer raises the question of what craft is and how does craft beer fit into a definition of craft. There is no easy answer to what craft is, and researchers tend to talk more about craft practices, rather than asking what craft is. DeNicola and Wilkinson-Weber (2016, p. 5) suggest, with a nod to Roland Barthes, that craft can function as an "empty signifier," and it points toward different forms of cultural disjunction. Sennett (2008) suggests that craft is based in skill and the craftsmanship begins after a person has put in a large number of hours to become really good at something. Quality is central to the idea of craft. Of course, this also implies that craft is handwork and is separated from mechanical work. This was probably something that was clearer at the beginning of the industrial age. It does seem clear that craft can be seen as a practice, a material engagement, and that scale does have something to do with the practice (Adamson, 2010).

When turning to beer, it is clear that some of these general ideas about craft certainly fit craft beer. In the early days, the brewing equipment was often handmade and out of the parts of other industries such as clothes washers, or dairy equipment. Over time, very professional brewing equipment has developed and so the idea that beer is "hand-crafted" takes on a bit different meaning. In some larger craft breweries, the brewing process is pretty automated. In smaller craft breweries, sacks of malt may still be manually dumped into the mash tun, even if there is some machine help. The Brewers Association (BA), the professional trade association of craft brewers, has a specific definition of the craft brewer. It involves seven elements of craft brewing. Craft brewing is small, innovative, traditional ingredients, community involvement, a close connection to customers, and independent from substantial investment by non-craft breweries (big beer) and local.[2] These elements themselves are somewhat fluid and in fact interestingly point to the cultural tensions within craft brewing. They are boundary markers for the community, and as such, they point to the risks to the community and the definition of craft at the boundary. They are not all problematic, but several point to major concerns.

If we start with the idea that craft brewing is small, that is a true statement. Craft beer accounts for 13.1% of the overall beer market by volume in 2021.[3] On one level that represents significant growth given where craft beer started, and for several years in the 2000s craft beer was the only segment of the beer market that was growing. Note that 13.1% of the volume of beer is small compared to the volume of beer produced by global industries like

AB InBev, the maker of Budweiser, Miller, and several other big beer labels. Originally, the BA defined small by the number of barrels of beer produced a year. As time went by, they had to increase that number, from 2 million barrels to 6 million barrels. Boston Beer Company, a company that has been part of the craft beer scene since the beginning but has always had a rocky relationship with craft beer, produced 8.5 million barrels in 2021. So, they stand outside this particular part of the definition of craft, and they recently merged with Dogfish Head Brewing, a well-loved craft brewery in Milton Delaware that is considered often part of the Philadelphia craft beer scene.

One could argue that 6 million barrels is still small compared to what "big beer" (an insider reference to companies like AB InBev) produces. At the same time, craft breweries started out by producing much smaller amounts of beer. For instance, in 2014 Bell's Brewery, no longer an independent brewery, produced 310,000 barrels in a year. By contrast, Yards Brewing, a pretty big craft brewery in Philadelphia, produced 55,000 barrels in 2015. And there are many smaller breweries in Philadelphia. While the 310,000 barrel number is well under the BAs definition, this could be considered a pretty big brewery operation. Some craft breweries are becoming large enough that we could consider them bigger businesses. And as bigger businesses, they become beholden to finance, mergers, take overs, etc.

Another key attribute of craft brewing is the idea of independence. The BA's definition of independent is, "Less than 25 percent of the craft brewery is owned or controlled (or equivalent economic interest) by a beverage alcohol industry member that is not itself a craft brewer." (See footnote 2 below.) From the beginning, craft brewing defined itself against what they call "big beer." By far, the image that comes to mind for craft beer people is that of AB InBev, and maybe even specific labels like Budweiser. These beers are considered "adjunct lagers" because they are brewed with adjunct sugars such as corn and rice. We will talk a bit more about adjuncts below. As early as the 1990s, beer critic Michael Jackson was criticizing the products of big beer as lacking in flavor, a conversation we will develop more in later chapters. Craft beer is independent because following the general idea of craft, quality is paramount. And the only way to guarantee integrity and quality is to be independent of larger financial influences that might trade profit over quality.

In 2017, the BA developed the independent seal, shown in Figure 1.2. Many readers may have seen this seal on their can or bottle of beer. The BA learned through a Harris poll that independent and independently owned were among the buzzwords that consumers were most aware of when associated with beer. Craft beer lovers share the dislike of big beer along with craft brewers. Independence is important because it is a potential sign of quality and proof that big beer has not interfered with the production of quality beer. While most craft breweries are still independent, there are an increasing number of larger craft breweries selling to big beer, and not just

*Figure 1.2* Brewers Association Independent Craft Brewer Seal

Source: Used by permission from the Brewers Association.

AB InBev but other international companies as well. This is a worry in the craft beer community. Some accept this as necessarily part of the evolution of craft beer and say that if the beer is still good, they don't care who owns it. But others worry that this is the beginning of compromising quality for the sake of profit, and that would lead to a decline of diversity in the beer market and the overall quality of beer.

Another key part of the definition of craft is the idea of traditional ingredients, initially meant to keep adjuncts out of craft beer. But one thing one can say about the craft brewing community is that they are very creative and experimental. In fact, one of the other key attributes, that craft brewers are innovative, has led to the inclusion of several different adjuncts in creative new craft beers. For the most part, these other adjuncts are not the ones used in adjunct lagers, but rather creative things like lactose sugar to make milkshake IPAs, and wine skins, and other fruits and fruit juices. The list just goes on. Five hundred years ago, the German Reinheitsgebot limited the ingredients that could be in beer to water, barley, and hops. The BA, in recognition that beer has a much longer history and many interesting ingredients in the past, decided they did not want to be the modern day Reinheitsgebot, but to open up to a larger set of ingredients. While the tension with big beer is very much felt around the idea of independence, the creative use of other ingredients is no longer felt to be a threat. People are not worried about the use of corn and rice adjuncts, because there is so much creative use of other ingredients. Traditional ingredients used to be another boundary marker that set craft off from big beer. And while small has continued to be an important boundary marker, even if small has been redefined, traditional ingredients are no longer perceived by the community as an important marker of what makes craft separate from big beer. Craft brewers are still very interested in quality ingredients, and so there is interest in organically grown grain, and small-batch malt production. There are strong environmental concerns for clean water and good growing environments for hops.

What has come to define craft beer is the creative uses of a wide variety of non-traditional and traditional ingredients. One could argue here that innovation became much more important to craft brewers and breweries than the use of traditional ingredients. This is also true for customers of craft beer. People who are interested in craft beer are on the lookout for new and interesting flavors. Creativity is highly valued. Not only are people interested in various kinds of additives, but also, they are very interested in different techniques such as fermenting beers in various kinds of whisky, wine, tequila oak casks, or the use of wild yeast varieties. The innovative use of techniques and ingredients continues to make craft beer stand out from big beer.

The other aspects of the BA's definition of a craft brewer, community involvement, a close connection to customers, and locality are still very important to many brewers and breweries. For many small to medium size breweries, up to 50% or more of their sales will happen in their tap room, or tap rooms if they have more than one. Craft beer consumers go on road trips to experience other breweries, beers, and the communities within which those beers are found. Craft beer fans will travel to locations for beers that are not distributed to their areas and then they will bring back some to give or trade with their friends. Craft breweries and brewpubs have brought back the idea of the neighborhood brewery for many communities. According to the BA, in 1980 there were 42 breweries in the United States. By 2018, there were over 6300, most of which were craft. Currently, there are 9118 craft breweries or brewpubs in the United States.[4] It has truly become a neighborhood phenomenon.

## Central Themes

So then, among the craft industries, we see craft beer as an important movement that raises several interesting questions about the potential for a socially balanced marketplace, the ways digital media allow smaller producers to thrive, and the process of how an industry is organized. We will talk about each of those themes in the book below, and the theories we have used related to these themes are developed in Chapter 2.

In his groundbreaking work on the rise of the market in Germany and its impact on democratic culture, Habermas (1989) suggested that the structural transformation of the economy, the rise of the market, created the context where there were newspapers, beer halls, cafes and more. These establishments fostered a democratic culture where people read the news, debated the issues in the beer halls and cafes, and contributed to a citizen's public discourse around the issues of the day. This is similar to Poster's (2001, p. 13) idea of the first media age that we discuss later in the book. Habermas then suggests that as capitalism continues to develop, social system becomes large and powerful and begins to colonize all aspects of public life, such that most of people's social activity occurs within the spaces of large corporations and there is little "public space" left. So, the system then undermines the democratic culture.

Poster and Habermas also frame this transformation around the rise of mass media and the creation of a passive receiving public. But one can also think about how a company like Starbucks, for example, began with the desire to bring the image of the Italian cafe to the American public. And the early Starbucks stores did indeed resemble a European cafe. But no one would mistake a modern Starbucks with its drive through, and its sugar and cream-laden drinks for a cafe. It is clearly the McDonalds of coffee-related beverages and cafe-related foods. While one could argue there is still a bit of democratic culture going on within a Starbucks store, one would have to say that the identities shaped by Starbucks are those of the mass consumer and uncritically consuming subject.

The craft beer movement returned us to the notion of the neighborhood pub. It is a place that is locally owned, it pays its workers more than large-scale industries do. More of the income and the profit remains in the community. The table in Figure 1.3 shows the growth of the number of breweries in the United States. In 2015, the number of craft breweries for the first time exceeded the number of breweries in the United States in the late 19th century.

The craft beer movement also reminded us that scale matters and that the market on a small scale can be prosocial. More recently, as craft beer has grown, the issue of scale has influenced the values that are core to craft beer. Are large craft breweries really "small"? Are they still community focused? As craft breweries get larger and the overall growth of the industry slows, we are starting to see more competition among breweries and less collaboration. This is an important tension in craft beer.

| Year | 2015 | 2016 | 2017 | 2018 | 2019 | 2020 | 2021 | 2020-2021 % change |
|---|---|---|---|---|---|---|---|---|
| **Craft** | **4803** | **5713** | **6661** | **7618** | **8419** | **8905** | **9118** | **4.4%** |
| Regional Breweries | 178 | 186 | 202 | 230 | 240 | 220 | 223 | 1.4% |
| Microbreweries | 2684 | 3319 | 3956 | 4518 | 1917 | 1898 | 1886 | -0.6% |
| Taprooms | | | | | 3091 | 3471 | 3708 | 6.2% |
| Brewpub | 1941 | 2208 | 2503 | 2870 | 3171 | 3302 | 3307 | 0.2% |
| Large Non-Craft | 44 | 67 | 106 | 104 | 111 | 120 | 129 | 7.5% |
| **Total U.S. Breweries** | **4847** | **5780** | **6767** | **7722** | **8530** | **9025** | **9247** | **2.5%** |

*Figure 1.3* Recent U.S. Brewery Count

Source: © Brewers Association.

A second critical theme is the question of the internet, digital, and social media. These electronic media are critical to the success of craft beer and have shaped important ideas like the idea that consumers (of craft beer) are also producers (of media that can be educational, valuable advertising, etc). Further, the brewers and the owners have depended on media to aid in the production, distribution, and marketing of their product. Digital media can gather specialty markets in a way that traditional mass media could not.

At the same time, digital media, by their capacity to transform spaces of interaction, help to create communities among producers and fans of craft beer. And these communities are rhizomatic in that they are local, regional, national, and overlapping (Deleuze & Guattari, 1987). The communities for craft beer not only play an important role in the economic activity in craft beer, but also an important role in the informal system of education and social reproduction. They help support home brewers as they learn the craft and as some home brewers transition to be craft brewers. And in terms of the discourse around social reproduction, craft beer forms an affinity space (Gee, 2005, 2009) as well as a community of practice, two concepts that might be seen as antagonistic but are in fact compatible. These are ideas that are explored later in the book.

A third theme in the book is the notion of value. Here we draw on the work of Graeber (2001, 2013) and the anthropological effort to reconcile the notions of values (as in community values) with the notion of economic value. Polanyi (1944), using anthropological research such as Malinowski's work on the Kula, suggested that there were two kinds of economics, formal economic and substantive economics. In traditional societies, there was no formal market, economic activity was woven throughout the rest of society, and the evolution of the market and formal economics was both a structural and historical development. Graeber moves from Polanyi's insight to drawing on the work of his mentors in economic anthropology to suggest that value is, across all kinds of societies, the human activity that is most important to members of that society. And the objects that that activity produces are both valuable and a fetish of the interaction itself. It is an object that is perceived to hold that value. We use Graeber's theoretical insights to understand that craft beer, and the culture of craft produces "value" that perhaps came very close to being more important than the value of money. This alternative set of values in craft beer makes it an interesting case for thinking about a more human-centered economy.

A final theme to mention here at the outset is the relationship of craft beer to capitalism, and the larger movements within consumer capitalism and consumer society in general. Most directly, craft beer has defined itself against what it calls "big beer," the large multinational conglomerates that produce the vast majority of beer sold worldwide. What makes craft, craft is that it is not big beer, it is small, community oriented, independent, etc. The large corporations that constitute big beer are very beholden to shareholders and for the most part are very distant from the craft of producing beer. And so, one could think of craft beer as being anti-capitalist in a sense that the community overall has been concerned to support values other than those of a very large profit-focused industry. One of our informants, early on in our research, suggested that Baltimore was ahead of Philadelphia in the early days of the craft beer movement. But according to the informant, the breweries in Baltimore were more competitive with each other, they behaved more like big beer, whereas the breweries in Philadelphia embraced the collaborative, community-oriented spirit. And so, the informant felt this is why breweries in Philadelphia surpassed those in Baltimore and Philadelphia became a more dynamic craft beer community while Baltimore did not. Whether there is truth in the story is not as important as the fact that it is a kind of cautionary tale to not be too much like big beer.

There is another level of craft beer's relationship to capitalism that we explore in the book as well. And that is that the evolution of consumer capitalism in the late 20th and early 21st centuries created an audience for craft beer and helped to create the spaces where craft beer could thrive. As the information revolution leads to the information society in the 1990s and 2000s, large and medium size cities, and even some small cities, become information hubs in the flow of information that makes the globalized economy run. And that has meant the cities have been reinvented as the old industrial city makes way for the new information city (Florida, 2002, 2005; Harvey, 2000, 2006; Lefebvre, 1991). Craft beer has benefited from this reorganization of cities in two ways. First, the old industrial landscape has created spaces for breweries and brewpubs. And these spaces were often less expensive and created a post-industrial landscape that had an aesthetic appeal. As this process continues, developers, very aware of the aesthetic appeal of these spaces, develop an urban entertainment landscape. While the price of real estate goes up with this process, it also brings in consumers who are looking for a craft experience and are seeking out coffee, wine, beer, and restaurants that are cutting edge. This consumer base will fuel the craft revolution. It is the very growth and transformation of the consumer culture and the consumer landscape that support the development of craft beer and gets it beyond its initial struggles of looking for a market.

## Chapters in the Book

The above themes find themselves the focus of particular chapters, but some of the themes cross several chapters. In Chapter 2, rather than focus on the central themes, we take up our own position in the research. We discuss how this research began as an interview project led by ethnographers, and how it more properly became an ethnography with some formal interviews as part of the process. Chapter 3 situates the craft beer study historically both the larger history of beer and the specific history in Philadelphia. While a whole book could be dedicated to the craft beer movement, and there are some we draw on, this chapter is designed to frame the larger political economy of craft beer that follows in Chapter 4. It is also designed to provide a historical framework for the study that is situated mostly in Philadelphia.

Chapter 4 looks at the political and economic context of craft beer. The chapter charts the shifts in capitalism from globalization and the information revolution to changes in consumer capitalism and the new place of cities. While looking at larger changes in consumer capitalism as they have impacted craft beer, the chapter also looks at the Philadelphia community. We further draw on some data from our research in the UK on craft brewing that creates a comparative context for the Philadelphia study. Chapter 5 looks at the ways that craft beer is really a knowledge industry and is based in the recipes, techniques, and experiences of brewing. The chapter explores notions of the invisible college, communities of practice, and affinity groups to think about the ways that knowing is organized and disseminated. It also looks at the ways in which expertise in the community is reproduced and how the community expands. Finally, the chapter recognizes that there are an increasing number of formal programs for training craft brewers, but the apprenticeship model is still the dominant form of education in the craft beer community.

Chapter 6 looks at how the internet and digital media are central to the development of the craft beer industry. Craft beer really begins in the 1980, but we could take it back to the late 1970s perhaps. This is the same period of time that microcomputing is beginning to grow. Microsoft and Apple were new companies in this era. The internet and the usenet were starting to become a household phenomenon. What the internet did for craft beer was make it possible to aggregate a market and support new interest in new kinds of beer without a huge amount of money spent on advertising and marketing. It also allowed brewers and new breweries to share their needs across the community for equipment, emergency loans of yeast and hops, etc. Digital media has really made "craft" possible, and this is true not only for beer, but for a number of other industries as well. Chapter 7 explores a key idea in the book and that is the notion of value and how the community focuses on values other than money. Craft beer is truly a craft industry as the quality of the product and the experience are more important, in some ways, than money. Money has to determine what the business does, but craft has driven the industry to not let money be the only value. We further discuss during the period of rapid growth in craft beer, the industry could be more idealistic about values of community and collaboration and perhaps now there is more of an instrumental shift toward competition.

Chapter 8 looks at some of the problems of the craft beer community. As researchers, we went into this work because we were interested in craft as a cultural phenomenon, and how it was an example of the current changes in consumer culture. Further, we were interested in the idealistic way craft brewers talked about their industry and their values. At the same time that there were all these positive things going on in the industry, there were clearly some social problems that we saw right away. Upon first looking into this culture, we were aware that this was a white male space, and that the industry was marked by whiteness. Further, and not surprisingly, as an alcohol-producing industry, issues of alcohol abuse were there too. These are research areas where we are not experts, but they were very clearly part of our ethnographic experience. Since our data collection, there has been increasing interest in why there are few breweries that are owned and run by people of color. There are a lot of popular press articles about Black breweries and non-white breweries, as well as breweries working with more people of color. We hope that these changes continue and it is clear that the Brewers Association, as the main professional association of craft beer, is very concerned about diversity. When we first began the study, there was also a "classic" gender breakdown in the industry with women in jobs that were more on the business side of the brewery (marketing, sales, and managing the pub) and men more involved in the brewing. That has begun to change thanks to the work of the Pink Boots Society and dedicated women in the industry.

In the conclusion, we summarize our thoughts across this range of concerns. We balance the ideal vision of craft beer with the limitations of it as a social movement. One the one hand, it is an exciting and progressive move in consumer culture as an industry with more concern for fair wages, community values, collaborating with each other, respect for the environment, and an overall concern with the quality of the product and the quality of the experience. On the other hand, that progressive vision is limited by both changes that are going on in the marketplace, as well as the racism, sexism and alcoholism that is part of the general social fabric.

## Notes

1 See this Huffington post article from 2014 for a nice assessment of the "hipness" of PBR. https://www.huffpost.com/entry/pbr-coolness-study_n_5399109

2 https://www.brewersassociation.org/statistics-and-data/craft-brewer-definition/
3 https://www.brewersassociation.org/statistics-and-data/national-beer-stats/
4 https://www.brewersassociation.org/association-news/importance-defining-small-independent/
https://www.brewersassociation.org/statistics-and-data/national-beer-stats/

## References

Adamson, G. (2010). Introduction. In G. Adamson (Ed.), *The craft reader* (pp. 1–5). Oxford, NY: Berg.

Deleuze, G., & Guattari, F. (1987). *A thousand plateaus: Capitalism and schizophrenia*. (B. Massumi, trans). Minneapolis, MN: University of Minnesota Press.

DeNicola, A. O., & Wilkinson-Weber, C. M. (2016). Introduction. In C. M. Wilkinson-Weber & A. O. DeNicola (Eds.), *Critical craft: Technology, globalization, and capitalism*. London: Bloomsbury (pp. 1–16).

Florida, R. L. (2002). *The rise of the creative class: And how it's transforming work, leisure, community and everyday life*. New York, NY: Basic Books.

Florida, R. L. (2005). *Cities and the creative class*. New York, NY: Routledge.

Gee, J. P. (2005). Semiotic spaces and affinity spaces. In D. Barton & K. Tusting (Eds.), *Beyond communities of practice: Language, power and social context* (pp. 214–232). Cambridge: Cambridge University Press.

Gee, J. P. (2009). Affinity spaces: From the age of mythology to today's schools. Retrieved from http://www.jamespaulgee.com/sites/default/files/pub/AffinitySpaces.pdf

Graeber, D. (2001). *Toward an anthropological theory of value: The false coin of our own dreams*. New York, NY: Palgrave Macmillan.

Graeber, D. (2013). It is value that brings universes into being. *HAU: Journal of Ethnographic Theory*, *3*(2), 219–243.

Habermas, J. (1989). *The structural transformation of the public sphere*. (T. Berger, trans.). Cambridge, MA: MIT Press.

Harvey, D. (2000). *Spaces of hope*. Berkeley, CA: University of California Press.

Harvey, D. (2006). Space as a keyword. In *Spaces of global capitalism: A theory of uneven geographical development* (pp. 119–148). London, NY: Verso.

Lefebvre, H. (1991). *The production of space*. Oxford: Basil Blackwell.

Polanyi, K. (1944). *The great transformation: The political and economic origins of our time*. Boston, MA: Beacon Press.

Poster, M. (2001). *What's the matter with the internet?* Minneapolis, MN: University of Minnesota Press.

Sennett, R. (2008). *The craftsman*. New Haven, CT: Yale University Press.

# 2 Brewing and Doing Ethnography

## Introduction

As researchers, we come from an anthropological tradition of ethnography. Shumar is a trained anthropologist. Mitman is a graduate of the Communication, Culture & Media (CCM) program at Drexel University where Shumar was a faculty member. The CCM program is an interdisciplinary program, but it has several anthropological ethnographers in the program and a strong ethnographic section in the program of which Mitman was a part with three of his main mentors being anthropologists. Anthropological ethnographers tend to be a bit different from ethnographers from other fields. One big difference is that they do not tend to see ethnography as a method, but rather see it as a practice of engagement with the "other" and with making sense out of the encounter. Further, there is a strong tendency in anthropology to see the limitations of the personal encounter we call ethnography. We will talk about this more below.

Although, as authors, we come from an ethnographic perspective, we did not originally see this study as an ethnography. Rather, we saw it as an interview study, where the interviews would be ethnographic in their orientation (Hockey & Forsey, 2012).[1] This was because neither of us felt we could fully immerse ourselves in the context and become participant observers. And in some ways, this was very true. If this study were a classic ethnography, it would have been nice to get jobs in breweries, particularly as brewers and spend a significant amount of time day-to-day in this practice. In that way, this was not a traditional ethnography. But as we discovered, there were other ways that the study, while retaining the interviews, became a more contemporary, or even postmodern ethnography. There are also elements of auto-ethnography in the work as well. Defining an encounter with "the other" in the contemporary world is itself a complicated task.

Early on in the research, we were presenting a paper on the craft beer study. At that point, the paper was about the theoretical framework we were using to discuss the importance of digital media, the production of forms of value, and the identities (prosumer) that were produced in this community. After the presentation and formal discussion, we engaged in an informal conversation

DOI: 10.4324/9781003109686-2

with a colleague who was a homebrewer and very interested in the work we were doing. He said to us, "you need to homebrew." He then proceeded to give us three reasons as to why we needed to homebrew. First, he felt we needed the experience in the practice, what it was like to be a brewer. Second, brewing would improve our interviews as we would share the problems and experiences with the professional brewers we were seeking to interview. Finally, the colleague suggested we were making too hard of a line separating homebrewers from craft brewers. He suggested that in fact that boundary was more fluid, and that people moved across that line regularly. So, early on in thinking about the study we were encouraged to problematize our position in the research, and our assumptions about who the "other" was.

While we did not go into this study to brew beer, we felt the truth of the advice our colleague gave us. In fact, it was very important advice and played a major role in making the study more ethnographic. As we began to brew beer, we learned about the important place of homebrew shops in the craft beer world. Homebrew shops could be thought of as the critical meeting place, a space where homebrewers and craft brewers came together. In fact, the early craft brewers in Philadelphia were connected to Home Sweet Homebrew, one of the original homebrew shops in the city.[2] We became a central part of a homebrew shop right outside the city lines of Philadelphia. Over our time as part of that homebrewing community, we watched three of the homebrewers open successful breweries. Two as a husband-wife team and the third person opened a brewery with another partner who was not part of the homebrew shop community. Further, we met a number of craft brewers through the shop and established a more detailed and informal relationship with these brewers beyond what one would expect from the relationship between interviewer and interviewee. As our work went on, we learned that most craft brewers started out as homebrewers and so the line that separates the two is indeed a blurry line.

## Boundaries

A set of issues we faced as anthropologically oriented ethnographers were how to think about the other. Craft beer is a social movement in the United States. But it is a social movement that is tied together with digital technology making it more than a traditional social movement. From the early days, craft brewers met with each other, worked to define the limits of craft beer. They shared needs and problems with each other. Some personalities conflicted. In a real way, one can say that craft beer is a national (and perhaps international) community of practitioners that share an imagined sense of being one group of people with a shared set of values, interests, knowledge, and practices (Anderson, 1991). And this study could have been attempted across multiple cities; however, it would be a much bigger and very different study.

There are also more local communities like the craft beer community in Philadelphia or San Diego or Chicago. Further, the communities have gotten even more fragmented. From our study in the Philadelphia area, we realized there are sub-communities that are mostly geographic areas to the north, southeast (New Jersey), and west of the city. And all these sub-communities are connected with each other and a larger national perspective, but disconnected from the larger community. They are more closely connected to the breweries and the people in their neighborhoods. In a real way, the Philadelphia community, like most craft beer communities in the United States (and elsewhere), is rhizomatic (Deleuze & Guattari, 1987). It is a set of overlapping semi-bounded groups that cluster together into a larger structure. For example, since the beginning, Dogfish Head was considered part of the Philadelphia community. This is in part because Sam Calagione was a colleague of other Philadelphia area brewers and got early supplies from Home Sweet Homebrew, a central meeting place of the craft beer movement in Philadelphia. But Dogfish Head is in Milton, Delaware, which is far from Philadelphia.

Brewing and becoming homebrewers allowed us to become immersed in the space in a way that a craft brewer might experience the space. We experienced the space as a Deleuzian assemblage. There were logical ways in which the different parts of the community (or communities) were connected. But then there was also a mental geography, where Downingtown, PA, Milton, DE, Philadelphia proper, and Cherry Hill, NJ, were overlapping spaces. Much of our ethnographic work ended up being in one part of the suburbs right outside of the city. Our interviews covered brewers, owners, and marketing representatives from all parts of the city. We did less ethnographic work in Britain where most of the work was based in interviews, and those interviews centered around York.

Philadelphia was a good city to focus on ethnography for craft beer. In many ways, it is a typical craft beer city. It had its firsts; Philly Beer Week was the first beer week of its kind and is the model for beer weeks in many other cities. There are well-known breweries in the Philadelphia area, and many smaller breweries. It may not be quite as famous as San Diego, Boston, Chicago, Seattle, but of course beer people will debate all these things.

There are a couple of other useful ways to think about the boundedness of our study and the ways in which there are overlapping and hybrid groupings. Gee (2005, 2009) has theorized the notion of what he calls "affinity groups" instead of communities of practice. For Gee, the affinity group is more about a shared set of interests, tastes, and values, and less about an actual community that is directly working together. Gee's work is an important part of understanding how people from very different places can share a set of attitudes, tastes and values, and even similar practices, but all at the same time not being part of a structured community. We will talk more about this idea in Chapter 5, as we think the craft beer movement involves both communities and affinity groupings. In fact, some of our informants, because of this notion of affinity groups, moved between craft-brewing communities in different cities and states. And so, the affinity grouping allowed them to move right into being a member of another community.

Cohen (1985) has suggested that boundaries between communities are symbolically constructed. Boundaries get enacted when they become important in symbolic interaction. And so, one does not think of oneself as American until one is either traveling to a different country or interacting with people from a different country. Then that boundary becomes significant. Similarly, boundaries within a locale, such as Philadelphia and its surrounding environs, become significant, in different ways, when interacting with others from different places. So, for local brewers, the distinction between Philadelphia proper, Valley Forge, Cherry Hill, Ardmore, and Berwyn are quite significant. Just the mention of Conshohocken, for example, will have locals thinking of different breweries and the strengths of those breweries. However, when talking to brewers and consumers in Seattle, these are all Philadelphia breweries. And there are some important ways in which they all embrace parts of a Philadelphia culture around craft brewing, which is a little more conservative, than the customs in Seattle. Cohen's point is that different boundaries get enacted in different moments and in different interactions. And, of course, the digital age complicates, in interesting ways, these enactments of boundaries. As the digital is able to warp space and time, the moments and interaction of boundary enactment can be quite complex and multiple. We will talk more about this idea in Chapter 6.

## Ethnography

In anthropology, ethnography is very closely associated with anthropological theory. Herzfeld (2001, p. 23), in his major work on anthropology, underscores the importance of relationship between anthropology and ethnography by stating:

> The very idea of separating ethnography from anthropology is to deprive it of its distinctive method, removing the source of its sole effective answer to the common charge that its studies are not representative of larger entities; namely, that what it loses in broad statistical replicability it gains in the sheer intensity of the ethnographic encounter – as intimacy, as privileged access, as listening to voices silenced on the outside by those who wield greater power.

Herzfeld refers to the work that anthropologists do as "the practice of theory" underscoring the fact that ethnographic fieldwork is not a "method" that can be abstracted from the experience of self and other that the ethnographer engages in. And so, Herzfeld (2001, p. 7) further states:

> Once we see theories as expressions of a social and political orientation and as heuristic devices for exploring social reality, rather than as the instruments of pure intellect, the theories become visible in hitherto unsuspected places. We begin to realize, in other words, that informants are themselves engaged in theoretical practices...

This update on the self/other encounter is hardly the language of positivist science and may have things in common with Latour's (1999) descriptions of the way science actually gets done but has little to do with the ways in which many in education conceive of scientific research.

Herzfeld's thinking about the "practice" that anthropologists engage in is related to some of the ideas that Katz and Csordas (2003) discuss in their work on phenomenological ethnography. While the goal of their article is specifically to look at the intersection between phenomenology and ethnography, in that encounter they make some important points that have bearing on the argument here. For instance, a part of their argument points to phenomenological ethnographic work that depends on a sense of embodiment in order to establish the ground of intersubjectivity in the self/other encounter (Katz & Csordas, 2003, p. 278). Central to Katz and Csordas's work is the idea that there is an ontological encounter between minds and bodies, that while experienced subjectively, is deeply real, and has important implications for the knowledge production process in ethnography. So that encounter is the opposite of an epistemological "method" where the corrupting influence of the body and subjectivity are held at bay as best as one possibly can.

Following on the phenomenological perspective and returning to Herzfeld, in his earlier work on "cultural intimacy," he suggests that the intimate nature of the ethnographic encounter is in fact akin to the forms of reliability that quantitative researchers seek in that the intimate encounter allows the ethnographer to engage with the "social poetics" of the informants. For Herzfeld, social poetics is a play of power that uses the poetics of everyday life to link to larger social narratives about nation and broader cultural ideals (Herzfeld, 1997, p. 25). This notion of poetics, while different, is related to Comaroff and Comaroff's (1987) use of the notion of poetics as a rhetorical way to explore and understand the world. Drawing on Mitchell's (1986) distinction between realist and rhetorical modes of representation and the linguistic anthropologist Friedrich (1979) ideas on the poetic, they suggest that first, the poetic is a legitimate way to explore the world and may in fact yield results that a more realist and scientific mode of representation cannot do. Thomas Mann said as much when he suggested that the novel, as a form for exploring the world, could indeed talk about things and present realities that are more difficult to do in non-fictional forms of representation. The Comaroff's, talking about the experiences of a brutal colonialism among the Tshidi people of South Africa, argue that the poetic was a way for local people to symbolically make connections between their village experiences and the exploitative practices of the colonial powers. These experiences are ones that are hard to make sense out of and so the poetic becomes a way, through symbol and metaphor, of forging their own theoretical practice.

In a related article, Ingold (2014, p. 384), echoing Herzfeld, suggests that ethnography is just "writing about the people." He further states, somewhat ironically:

> And, we are equally entitled to protest when those who assess our own proposals demand of us, in the name of ethnography, the same slavish adherence to the protocols of positivist methodology, by requiring us to specify—for example—how many people we intend to talk to, for how long, and how they will be selected.
>
> (Ingold, 2014, p. 384)

Ingold goes on to say, very eloquently, what most anthropologists would say, when asked what they do. He suggests that anthropology is an encounter with the other. And that encounter involves the whole-body experience of attempting to understand the other and the world they are both part of and in the process of producing. Luvaas (2022) reminds us that in that encounter with the other, they are in the midst of not just living in the world, but also the daily creative practice of bringing their world into being. Life is a process and ethnography is not "capturing data" but rather a sharing in that process, and a "making sense" of that experience.

## Positivist Science

In contrast to this anthropological perspective on ethnography, positivism focuses on method and methodology. This is not a new idea nor am I the first to suggest such a notion. Bourdieu and Wacquant make a similar assertion when he suggests that American sociology was dominated in the postwar period by Parsons, Merton, and Lazarsfeld. Bourdieu and Wacquant, with their concern to return to concrete embodied practices and to approach them sociologically, requires that theory and method are not separated from each other. Further, they suggest that one strand of American sociology, with the empirical use of large data sets, is a complete pre-occupation with methodology devoid of theory (Bourdieu & Wacquant, 1992).

Positivism from its beginnings asserts that one cannot approach reality directly. Consequently, the only possible avenue for scientific understanding is epistemological. And by engaging in a precise definition of the concepts used and the removal of the subjectively tainted researcher through large data sets, double blind experiment, matched control groups only then can we have some hope of scientific understanding.

A further problem with positivism is its view of the world that is simplistic and under theorized. Reality is seen as sets of facts and the scientific method can be used to understand the connections between facts and produce, for example, covering laws. While this view of science has been adequately critiqued in the philosophy of science, it is still a dominant ideology in the practice of science in many scientific disciplines. It's not that contemporary social scientists would specifically adhere to the principles of positivism, but there is a strict adherence to the principle of rigor in methods that positivism brought to the social sciences, hence Ingold's above criticism of reviewers not understanding what anthropologists are doing.

Further, while post-positivists would argue it is true one cannot escape subjective tainting of the data by the research, the goal is still a methodological rigor to minimize the impact of subjectivity.

The further elaboration of method creates complex protocols that in themselves become very complex and difficult to follow and ironically require significant subjective interpretation in simply following the protocol (Brandt, 2008). Further, this is the discovery that Latour and Woolgar (1979) made early in their work that the protocols in science were so complex that people had to develop a "feel" for the data and what data to keep and what data to throw out. This has led Latour (1999) to his later work where he sees the production of the object of science part of the research process itself, which is not a postmodern denial of reality but a recognition that the complex nature of reality is such that positive science tends to carve out specific pieces of the real in and then make claims about that world.

In the social sciences, both sociology and psychology have been heavily dominated, at least in the United States, by a positivist orientation that is focused on methodological training (Bourdieu & Wacquant, 1992, p. 225) and the answering of discrete research questions with robust methodology and less concern with theory. This emphasis has led to a further reifying of methodological practices as the "gold standard" for reliable and accurate research with little thinking about the philosophical implications of such a focus.

## Counter Narratives and Trends

Qualitative researchers have always had to fight for their epistemological positions in the social sciences. Our concern here is not to question the value of a lot of qualitative[3] work in the social sciences but rather to talk specifically about the transformation of ethnography in this political/economic context in the social sciences. In much social scientific research, we could characterize the discussion of ethnography as falling into three discursive moments. These discursive moments are not exactly historically linear, and there is a lot of overlap. We could think of them as logical moments. In the first moment, the discussion focused on the opposition between quantitative versus ethnography. Ethnography was seen as not scientific, especially in anthropology. And if we look at the work of Malinowski, he saw ethnography as something of a cross between a science and literature. In fact, many anthropological textbooks say that anthropology, (meaning cultural anthropology), is a cross between a scientific and a humanities discipline. So, in this discursive moment, ethnographic research was seen as weak and unscientific. It did not have the methodological rigor of quantitative research. In *The Ethnographer's Magic*, Stocking (1992) discussed the way the phenomenological "being there" was a kind of magic that gave the ethnographic encounter its rigor but did not line up with scientific ideas about methodological rigor.

This first moment yielded to a second discursive moment where there was a concerted effort to make ethnography, and other qualitative research more scientific. There was a tendency to focus on methods and to develop different methodological protocols. One hallmark of this moment was the idea of "mixed methods," which were hailed as a way to get past the impasse of quantitative versus qualitative (Cresswell, 2003). In that moment, ethnographic research was seen as the handmaiden of quantitative research offering things like hypothesis generation, theory building, and in-depth samples. These offerings were seen as enhancements to the rigor of quantitative research. Here qualitative research techniques like ethnography can explore the social world to help theory development. This work then feeds the "gold standard" research where we move to the deductive phase of large-scale quantitative hypothesis testing.

The third discursive moment espouses a greater sense that research methods should be chosen based on the kinds of research questions that are being asked or the research problems that are being addressed, rather than only trying to merge quantitative and ethnographic/qualitative in a more general way (Nathan & Jackson, 2006). In this view, ethnographic and qualitative research may stand on their own and not be the handmaid of quantitative research. It simply depends on what one is looking at. While qualitative methods have gained their "freedom" through the struggles with being seen as less scientific than quantitative methods, the culture in the study of qualitative methods has taken on the idea that there needs to be scientific justification for the use of ethnography and a specific protocol for how to do ethnographic research. Rigor is now a concept that many qualitative researchers have embraced.[4] While this most recent trend in qualitative thinking, largely outside of anthropology, could be seen as positive development, we have come a long way from the idea that ethnography is a form of writing, a literature. It is no longer seen by many as an encounter with the other, but rather a rigorous method for gaining access to the subjective experience of social actors. And this further leads to Ingold's frustration that scholars outside of the discipline of anthropology are now suggesting that he does not have the rigor necessary for good ethnographic research. Ethnography, in its various forms, becomes another set of methodological tools for getting at a post-positivist reality. And lost are Ingold and Herzfeld's ideas that ethnography is an encounter with some "other" and a process of the "practice of theory."

While we are characterizing this discourse around ethnography and qualitative work as a set of moments, we would hasten to add that these moments are in fact conceptual planes and are in part related to a temporal unfolding but not completely. As in all political struggles, time and discourse fold in on each other and stretch out such that delineating precise boundaries is difficult.[5] Further, we are not suggesting that quantitative research methodologies are not valuable. Rather, like Bourdieu, we would suggest that the separation of theory and method are at the core of a mistaken set of procedures in the social sciences. Our concern in this chapter is with what we, and other anthropologists see as the distortion to ethnography. And further, that distortion is important here, as we seek to articulate a set of theoretical interpretive frames that frame our "practice of theory" (Herzfeld, 2001).

In the 1980s, Baudrillard (1983) suggested that the Americans had won the Vietnam War. He stated that even though America officially lost, the goal was to take a truly different society, the other, and remake it in the image of the self, in this case American capitalism. Baudrillard could not have been more right. Now nearly 50 years after the end of that war, Vietnam is a paragon of consumer capitalist innovation. As the tourists from the United States and elsewhere travel over the Vietnamese landscape, they encounter a commodified and re-imagined history design specifically for the export market (Schwenkel, 2006).

In the same way, we would suggest that while ethnography has gained a lot of ground in the social sciences over the 20th and early 21st centuries, it has lost the war. In the process of engagement with the dominant forms of positivist and post-positivist research in the social sciences, ethnography has become a method in the struggle. And the most important part of becoming a method in this struggle is that ethnographic researchers have engaged in a methodological fetishism elaborating more and diverse "qualitative methods," attempting a kind of rigorous methodological parallel to quantitative methods. In our work, we return to a more anthropological view of ethnography. And here we would argue, with Ingold, that we have spent a lot of time brewing beer, and interacting with brewers and other individuals related to the brewing process. We have hung out with the community, worried about when our yeast stalls, and what to do with bad batches of beer. In this encounter, we have become part of the craft brewing community and the line between ourselves as social scientists and as brewers has become blurred.

As Luvaas (2019) points out, this is not uncommon among ethnographers. Part of being with the other involves a becoming with the other. For Luvaas, this becoming both blurs the line between what people call autoethnography and ethnography. And following Luvaas, we find we have followed his three stages of becoming, without knowing it. We began as consumers of craft beer and became more sophisticated consumers. We were then encouraged to become producers and we not only produced beer, but we then went on to be part of the community, submitting beers to beer competitions, participating in large social events, and contributing to the media world of craft beer with our social reviews and virtual presence at large social events. And so, elements of our study were still rooted in the interviews we did. The study became ethnographic and autoethnographic as we got deeper into the practice of brewing and participating in the community.

## Theoretical Practice

Finally, we turn to theory. As the reader will see in the following chapters, different theoretical frames help guide the work and make sense of the craft beer communities in which we have participated. As we stated in Chapter 1, initially we were guided by a sense that craft beer was about other forms of value than those that one typically sees in the consumer capitalist marketplace. And we were interested in the way this craft community worked to elevate craft values, along with other social values such as environmentalism and fair labor. We were also interested in the ways that social media supported the development of this alternative industry. Further, as time goes by, we see that there was a golden age where craft was about these alternative values but as it has become more successful and grown, the market and finance have become increasingly more important and are starting to crowd out these other values. And perhaps this is creating a split in the craft beer community with smaller more community-oriented breweries and pubs and bigger more market-oriented breweries. Here we will briefly overview the main theories that we have used to make sense of our experience, and more details on the theoretical frames will be developed in the different chapters.

We can think of our theoretical framework as having four main perspectives, political economy, media, community & social reproduction, and value. The first perspective focuses on the transformation of global capitalism and the development of consumer capitalism in the post 1960s era. Ethnographies in recent decades, from an anthropological perspective, have tended to frame the local within and nation and international political economy. In the current era, one cannot fully understand what is going on at this local level without an understanding of the locale within a global framework. To think about political economy, we have focused on the work of David Harvey, Michel Aglietta, Grant McCracken, Giovanni Arrighi, and others. These thinkers, tending to come from a Marxist perspective, are focused on the ways in which global capitalism is contradictory and how the current arrangement of productive and consumptive relations are the result of temporary resolutions to early contradictions. The stagnation of consumer capitalism in the 1970s, for instance, led to not only the rise of neoliberalism, and the liberation of the financial system, but also the spatial transformations of productive relationships and what Harvey (1989) called "flexible accumulation."

Flexible accumulation was only possible due to changes in the transportation and communication infrastructure. And these changes led to not only global cities (Sassen, 2001) but also cities where information work was more central, and a professional class was doing the work in an information economy. As Florida (2005) pointed out, the professional class was seeking new forms of entertainment and they fueled the rise of cafes, craft brewpubs, wine bars, arts, etc. Not only were these relationships central to larger cities, but every city became an island of cosmopolitan culture, rather than a site of industrial production as it was in a previous generation. Upmarket consumers enjoyed the irony that farm to table restaurants and craft breweries replaced the mill as the central focus of the town, very often literally by occupying the mill building.

Even more contemporary perspectives, such as those advocated by Deleuze and Guattari (1987), are really a macrostructural framing of how these unusual relationships end up in close proximity to each other. The assemblage is itself a product of globalization that has brought together different borders creating relations of externality. Deleuze and Guattari focus on the fact that this creates sets of relations of externality and are different from previous eras when we might think about the internal organization of a city. Another related perspective is Appadurai's (1990) notion of disjuncture. For Appadurai, there are different "scapes," a metaphor taken from landscape. These scapes are composed of people, media images, capital, data, materials, etc. They flow through different sites, or nodes in different volumes based on their own specific criteria, that is, where they come from and where they are going. And any city or town is then again a set of external relations these scapes come into contact with each other not due to some internal logic of the place, but rather by the chance encounter of where they are headed. And as such they come to define a particular place in some important ways.

Media has played a large part in the political and economic transformations discussed in our first theoretical perspective. A big part of Harvey's flexible accumulation is the communication infrastructure that has made the transformation possible. This would include satellite technologies, communication infrastructure, personal computers, handheld technologies, the internet, and more recently social media. While many researchers today focus on social media and its impact on our social lives, it is only the most recent set of tools from the whole evolution of the communication environment. We draw on Poster's (2001 important work on the internet. While it was earlier work and largely forgotten, Poster critically addresses the relationship of subjects to the media era. Poster argues that if print media was part of the construction of the modern independent subject who would read, discuss, and make decisions, and if the era of broadcast media brought about an anxiety about that subject who could no longer read and determine, but only watch, listen, and passively receive (Horkheimer & Adorno, 1947/2002), then the internet brought the individual into the communication spaces itself, transforming the subject as another node in the network of media interactions. In this way, the line between actor and actant becomes blurred as does producer and consumer. The internet, with its endless stream of digital objects that can be worked and reworked, made the craft beer revolution possible. Everyone becomes a messenger, an advertiser in this medium. And all become community members as they participate in the craft beer community. Here we see that Ritzer and Johansen's notion of prosumption is very important. The craft beer movement has been fueled by the fact that the line between producer and consumer has become blurred. Similarly, Neff's (2012) notion of venture labor, and Duffy's (2017) notion of aspirational labor are also very useful for thinking about the work that gets done in the craft beer community and the ways that individual work to support the success of craft as a community in different ways, some formal with pay, others informal with less or no pay. And finally, while the internet makes it possible for all of us to be nodes in the network, Boellstorff's (2008) gap between the actual and the virtual are significant for creating a sense of belonging and a sense that there is a community to be part of.

A very important part of craft beer in the United States is the way in which knowledge and learning the craft was communicated. While there are more formal institutions focusing on training craft brewers now, most craft brewers learned the trade by first becoming homebrewers and then apprenticing at a brewery where they learned to brew on a larger scale, as well as other aspects of the industry. This leads to two observations, first, one homebrew shop supplier referred to home brewing as the "invisible college" of the craft beer industry. The idea of the invisible college in Europe began when a group of natural philosophers formed around the figure of Robert Boyle. This group of scholars, the beginnings of more modern sciences, was somewhat at odds with the traditional scholars of Oxford and Cambridge. And so they began as an informal group that later became the Royal Society of London. The idea that brewers were not part of a formal society but began as an informal collection of experts who educated each other in the brewing sciences naturally led to this designation of an invisible college.

A second observation is that craft brewing is really a community of practice model (Lave & Wenger, 1991). It's a little hard to think about the "community" in the CoP model for the reason discussed above about space. But certainly, local breweries were CoPs and sometimes local communities of brewers who got together to talk beer were CoPs. But there is even a sense that the CoP operated on regional and national scales at meetings and competitions. Again, we develop this idea of the community of practice to think about the ways that brewers are organized. We also compare the notion of a CoP with the related idea of an affinity group (Gee, 2005, 2009). Affinity groups are people who share interests, tastes, values, and practices, but are not actually a formal group. We suggest that both concepts explain the organization of brewers, sometimes they are part of a local or regional community of practice, and other times they might see themselves as part of a larger national, or even international affinity group.

In our work, a central theoretical construct motivating our thinking is the notion of value. Anthropologist Graeber (2001, 2013) did groundbreaking work by reconciling the notion of cultural values, with the notion of economic value. Polanyi (1944), in *The Great Transformation* began this work of reconciling values with value by pointing out that traditional societies did not have a separate arena called the economic, but rather economic activity was tied up with other central symbolic activities in that society. We can think of Malinowski's (1922) discussion of Kula in Trobriand society. Polanyi saw the formal economy as something that was both a historical moment, and something of a reification in modern societies. Graeber (2001) points out that this work was more or less dropped in anthropology and the problem was never completely solved.

While Graeber's theory is quite involved, he essentially came to the point that "value" is the result of human interactions that are considered most important in a society and the objects related to that human activity come to hold "the value" of that interaction. This is both a reification and a fetish in the classic Marxist sense of these terms. In an important way, Graeber's work on value helps us to understand some seemingly irrational aspects of modern capitalism. For instance, why do billionaires continue to amass billions of dollars when that amount of money becomes so great that it starts to be meaningless. But if we compare the game of finance, with Kula[6] as a social game, then we can see that this is about forms of (largely male) status and it is the cultural game that members of this cultural community play. It's not about some middle-class notion of being able to buy a summer home and a new car.

The craft beer community, at its idealistic zenith, was about a different set of ultimate values. And the value of capital accumulation was subordinated to the higher value of craft. A metaphor of this moment was the famous Collaboration not Litigation beer, where Avery Brewing and Russian River Brewing decided to collaborate on a beer rather than compete when each brewery noticed they had a beer with the same name. This decision in 2006 was a sign that craft beer was about community, quality, collaboration, and other pro-social values. For us, it is one of the main reasons we began studying craft beer. This was a community that was about producing a traditional economic product but was seemingly not about chasing after money and capital accumulation.[7] The status game in this community, at that moment, seemed to be about other things. There was certainly significant status competition. Brewers competed to create the best beers, and to invent new beer styles. Especially in the United States, brewers were seeking to make big beers in terms of flavor and alcohol by volume (ABV). But the quest for quality of product, a good drinking experience, sharing in a community, and caring about workers and the environment were all central parts of the craft beer community and the interactions in craft beer. This was perhaps a special moment where an industry could explore other forms of value.

As craft beer became more successful and developed more of an audience, it became easier to not focus on the money and to see craft beer as more caught up in a "higher" set of values. At the same time, more venture capitalists were interested in investing in more breweries and so the interests of money also increased during this time. Figure 2.1 is a graph of the growth of craft beer. By about 2015, the tremendous growth of craft beer slowed down and production

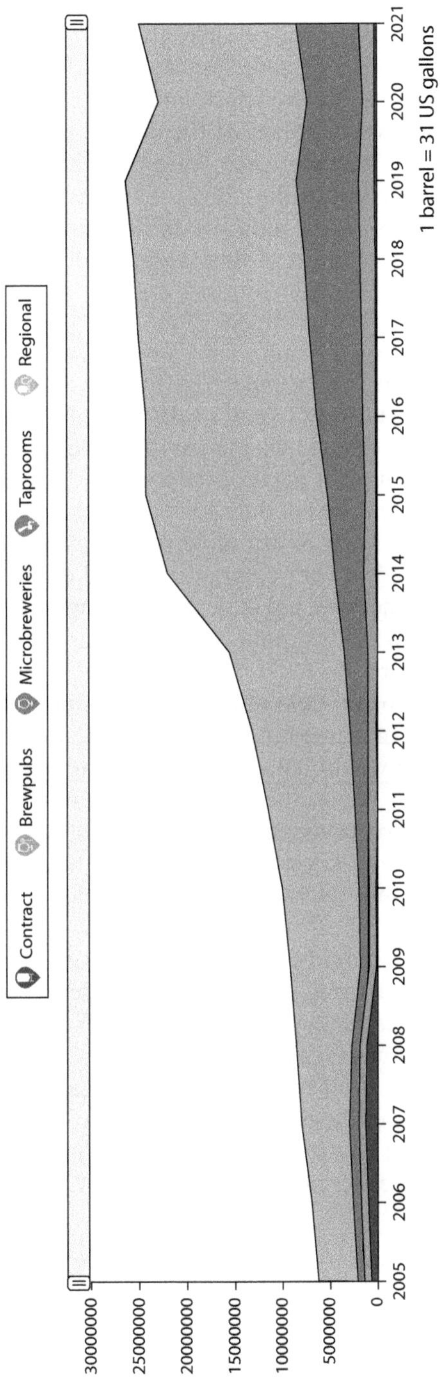


*Figure 2.1* Historical Craft Brewery Production by Category

Source: © Brewers Association.

by volume began to flatten out at the same moment that some big breweries became big. At this point, the quest after alternative values slowed down.

What we see today are some big breweries that are very focused on finance and the bottom line, while some brewpubs and smaller breweries are still holding up an alternative set of values as the dominant values. This situation is likely to continue. Recently, there have been a series of litigations over trademarks and labels (Thornley, 2017). This has upset much of the craft beer community but is a good indicator of the values shift. We discuss these issues of value and the context of value creation in detail in Chapter 7.

## Limitations

All ethnographic work has limitations. And further, knowledge is often advanced through making mistakes. In our early efforts to understand what was going on in Philly Beer Week, we missed many opportunities to meet with well-known brewers in other parts of the country. In some cases, those missed opportunities led to different unexpected opportunities. Sometimes they just led to missing an event or not understanding where an event was taking place. We competed in beer competitions and even earned a third place in the first round of the National Homebrew Competition. At the same time, we had several batches of beer that were utter failures. Overall, we did not become the best brewers.

Some mistakes have to be thought of as the limitation of the work itself. As we began to get more immersed in the community, we had less time to do formal interviews. We would have liked to have done more interviews with brewers and owners. But at the same time, the number of informal conversations at beer conventions, educational events, tastings, and competitions greatly increased our knowledge. When an ethnographer becomes more immersed in a community, there is often a trade-off between depth and breadth of experience.

As we continued to brew more beer and work at getting good at the practice, this led to the transition from just researcher to research and brewer. At points in the research, we were very much more brewer and not thinking of ourselves as researchers. Luvaas (2019, p. 247) suggests that our informants are engaged themselves in a self-project, they are engaged in a process of becoming. And we too, as ethnographers, joined them in that process. We are still very much focused on being brewers and don't really see an end to that practice, an enduring effect of the research project.

## Notes

1 Overall, we did 23 formal interviews. Nineteen of them were in the United States and 4 were in the UK. Shumar, as lead author, did other research in Denmark during the time of this study. And while we did not interview brewers or other craft beer persons in Denmark, we did get a close look at the craft beer community there and talked with brewpub personnel and staff at craft beer

bottle shops. The interviews were primarily with brewers and brewer/owners. We also interviewed owners, marketing representatives, educators, bar owners, and other shop owners. Some people had more than one of these roles.

2 https://www.homesweethomebrew.com/our-story.htm

3 In fact, the very term qualitative research or qualitative methods may in fact have developed from the opposition between more traditional forms of ethnography and positivist research. In order to help ethnography gain legitimacy, the term "qualitative methods" is a product of the struggle with positivism. See Brinkmann, Jacobsen, and Kristiansen's (2014) Historical Overview of Qualitative Research in the Social Sciences.

4 We want to be clear that we do not see the historical developments in qualitative research as a bad thing. Increased rigor when doing focus groups, interview studies, and other kinds of qualitative methods can be very good. Our concern is with the transformation of ethnography, and the critique (or maybe better stated as a lack of understanding) of the anthropological practice of ethnography or maybe what Herzfeld and perhaps Ingold might like to call "doing anthropology."

5 For instance, it was not that long ago that the ideas of the "free market" and neoliberal economic ideology were seen as hopelessly out-of-date and wrong. No one in 1965 would have imagined that these ideas could again have any currency. And yet they are now seen as not only legitimate but that there has been a logical historical unfolding of the value of the free market.

6 For readers not familiar with the Kula exchange, this is a system of ritual exchange discussed by Malinowski (1922) in his ethnography Argonauts of the Western Pacific. In the book, Malinowski talks about how Kula is a system of ritual exchange of valuable necklaces and armbands among people on the islands off the eastern tip of New Guinea.

7 Of course, there are lots of caveats here. Craft beer is not the first commodity to attempt a more socially and environmentally responsible business. In the 1990s, responsible consumerism was an important movement perhaps most famously represented by Ben & Jerry's. Further, in the current moment, the craft movement goes way beyond beer and there are a lot of other industries, for example, wine, coffee, food, and other crafts, that also attempt to elevate other values beyond just making money. Finally, as we will point out in later chapters, 2008–2015 was perhaps craft beer's golden era when growth was dramatic and worry about competition and the "bottom line" was something owners and brewers could worry about less.

## References

Anderson, B. R. O. G. (1991). *Imagined communities: Reflections on the origin and spread of nationalism* (Rev. extended ed.). New York, NY: Verso.

Appadurai, A. (1990). Disjuncture and difference in the global cultural economy. *Public Culture*, *2*(2), 1–24.

Baudrillard, J. (1983). *Simulations*. New York, NY: Semiotext(e).

Boellstorff, T. (2008). *Coming of age in second life: An anthropologist explores the virtually human*. Princeton, NJ: Princeton University Press.

Bourdieu, P., & Wacquant, L. J. D. (1992). *An invitation to reflexive sociology*. Chicago, IL: University of Chicago Press.

Brandt, C. B. (2008). Protocols and performances: Scientific discourse in the molecular biology laboratory. In J. E. Canaan & W. Shumar (Eds.), *Structure and agency in the neoliberal university*. New York, NY: Routledge.

Brinkmann, S., Jacobsen, M. H., & Kristiansen, S. (2014). Historical overview of qualitative research in the social sciences. In P. Leavy (Ed.), *The Oxford handbook of qualitative research*. Oxford: Oxford University Press.
Cohen, A. P. (1985). *The symbolic construction of community*. New York, NY: Routledge.
Comaroff, J., & Comaroff, J. L. (1987). The madman and the migrant: Work and labor in the historical consciousness of a South African people. *American Ethnologist*, *14*(2), 191–209.
Cresswell, J. W. (2003). *Research design: Qualitative, quantitative, and mixed methods approaches*. Thousand Oaks, CA: Sage Publications.
Deleuze, G., & Guattari, F. (1987). *A thousand plateaus: Capitalism and schizophrenia*. (B. Massumi, trans.). Minneapolis, MN: University of Minnesota Press.
Duffy, B. E. (2017). *(Not) getting paid to do what you love: Gender, social media, and aspirational labor*. New Haven, CT: Yale University Press.
Florida, R. L. (2005). *Cities and the creative class*. New York, NY: Routledge.
Friedrich, P. (1979). *Language, context, and the imagination*. (Selected and Introduced by Anwar S. Dil). Stanford, CA: Stanford University Press.
Gee, J. P. (2005). Semiotic spaces and affinity spaces. In D. Barton & K. Tusting (Eds.), *Beyond communities of practice: Language, power and social context* (pp. 214–232). Cambridge: Cambridge University Press.
Gee, J. P. (2009). Affinity spaces: from the age of mythology to today's schools. Retrieved from http://www.jamespaulgee.com/sites/default/files/pub/AffinitySpaces.pdf
Graeber, D. (2001). *Toward an anthropological theory of value: The false coin of our own dreams*. New York, NY: Palgrave Macmillan.
Graeber, D. (2013). It is value that brings universes into being. *HAU: Journal of Ethnographic Theory*, *3*(2), 219–243.
Harvey, D. (1989). *The condition of postmodernity*. Oxford: Basil Blackwell.
Herzfeld, M. (1997). *Cultural intimacy: Social poetics and the nation-state*. New York, NY: Routledge.
Herzfeld, M. (2001). *Anthropology: Theoretical practice in culture and society*. Malden, MA: Blackwell Publishers.
Hockey, J., & Forsey, M. (2012). Ethnography is not participant observation: Reflections on the interview as participatory qualitative research. In J. Skinner (Ed.), *The interview: An ethnographic approach* (pp. 69–87). New York, NY: Bloomsbury.
Horkheimer, M., & Adorno, T. W. (2002). *Dialectic of enlightenment: Philosophical fragments* (E. Jephcott, trans.). Stanford, CA: Stanford University Press. (Original work published 1947).
Ingold, T. (2014). That's enough about ethnography! *HAU: Journal of Ethnographic Theory*, *4*(1), 383–395.
Katz, J., & Csordas, T. J. (2003). Phenomenological ethnography in sociology and anthropology. *Ethnography*, *4*(3), 275–288.
Latour, B. (1999). *Pandora's Hope. Essays on the reality of science studies*. Cambridge, MA; London, England: Harvard University Press.
Latour, B., & Woolgar, S. (1979). *Laboratory life: The construction of scientific facts*. Beverly Hills, CA: Sage Publications.
Lave, J., & Wenger, E. (1991). *Situated learning: Legitimate peripheral participation*. Cambridge, England; New York, NY: Cambridge University Press.

Luvaas, B. (2019). Unbecoming: The aftereffects of autoethnography. *Ethnography, 20*(2), 245–262.

Luvaas, B. (2022). Shadow worlding: Chasing light in Yogyakarta. *American Anthropologist, 124*, 399–416.

Malinowski, B. (1922). *Argonauts of the Western Pacific: An account of native enterprise and adventure in the archipelagos of Melanesian New Guinea*. London: Routledge & Sons.

Mitchell, W. J. T. (1986). *Iconology: Image, text, ideology*. Chicago, IL: University of Chicago Press.

Nathan, M., & Jackson, K. (2006). Reframing the role of Boolean classes in qualitative research from an embodied cognition perspective. In S. Barab, K. Hay, & D. Hickey (Eds.), *Proceedings of the international congress of the learning sciences* (pp. 502–508). Mahwah, NJ: Erlbaum.

Neff, G. (2012). *Venture labor: Work and the burden of risk in innovative industries*. Cambridge, MA: MIT Press.

Polanyi, K. (1944). *The great transformation: The political and economic origins of our time*. Boston, MA: Beacon Press.

Poster, M. (2001). *What's the matter with the internet?* Minneapolis, MN: University of Minnesota Press.

Sassen, S. (2001). *The global city: New York, London, Tokyo* (Rev. ed.). Princeton, NJ: Princeton University Press.

Schwenkel, C. (2006). Recombinant history: Transnational practices of memory and knowledge production in contemporary Vietnam. *Cultural Anthropology, 21*(1), 3–30.

Stocking, G. W. Jr. (1992). *The ethnographers magic and other essays in the history of anthropology*. Madison, WI: University of Wisconsin Press.

Thornley, D. (2017). Litigation, not collaboration: The changing landscape of trademark disputes in the craft-beer industry. *Marquette Intellectual Property Law Review, 21*. Available from https://scholarship.law.marquette.edu/iplr/vol21/iss2/6

# 3 History of Craft Beer

## Introduction

As we have discussed in preceding chapters, the work in this book is primarily centered in one city and its environs in the United States that has evolved a craft beer culture that is both particular to itself, but in many ways very much like other craft beer cities in the United States. As such the core of this chapter focuses on the history of craft beer as it relates to Philadelphia and the Philadelphia region. By comparison, we are also looking at the rise of craft beer in Britain. Craft beer in Britain has had a very different history because the larger history of beer has been so different than in the United States. The larger historical context of these two nations allows for a very interesting contrast of the history of craft beer as well as the imagination of the place of beer in nested range of contexts, the national culture, the regional culture, and the place of beer in local communities. To broaden the comparative picture, we will also talk a little bit about the history of craft beer in Denmark and Japan, two places where craft beer's impact has been very significant. Of course, there are many other places we could discuss, but that would have to be the focus of a different book.

## Imagination

The history of prohibition and the continued consolidation of breweries in the aftermath of prohibition is often portrayed as a negative period of time for beer by craft beer enthusiasts. The period not only involved a reduction of the number of breweries in cities and in the United States in general, it also was a time when the neighborhood brewery and brewpub disappeared. But at the same time, this history created a very important context for American craft beer. With a history more or less wiped out, American brewers were free to be forward looking and imagine beer in new ways. And while the first generation of craft breweries revived the older tradition of German lagers that began to dominate the American market by the mid-19th century (Stack, 2003), later generations of craft brewers were forward-looking. They began to not only brew other European styles of beer but felt free to creatively embellish those traditional styles. This is probably most clearly seen

DOI: 10.4324/9781003109686-3

in the various versions of the American IPA that while loosely based on the traditional British IPAs, is a genuinely unique beer.

By contrast, the craft beer movement in Britain fights against a general beer culture that is more backward-looking, more bound by tradition. Sometimes the CAMRA movement is compared to the craft movement as both movements are concerned with local beer, small-scale production, and quality ingredients. But CAMRA is motivated by a getting back to the truth of real ale, a rich and noble history of British beer making. Craft beer, with its forward-looking nature and creative recipes, has had a harder time gaining traction in this nation with a sense of the history of good beer. Craft beer as a movement does develop in Britain, but it follows on the heels of the CAMRA movement. Further, because beer has been more central to British culture, the craft beer movement in Britain developed slowly, and was in a sense attempting a merger between American craft beer and "real ales." This led to craft beer getting a much slower start in Britain and did not really develop until the craft beer scene was fully developed in the United States. For narrative clarity, this chapter will focus on the history of craft beer in the United States. We will discuss the history of craft beer in Britain in the next chapter (Chapter 4) as it fits well with the political economy of beer in Britain.

Beer is also an object onto which people tend to project ideas about the community, the region, and the nation. Breweries and local pubs in the past became a central part of many communities. As we said above, in 19th century Philadelphia there were several hundred breweries, and each served the neighborhood in which it was found. The pub became a part of community life and was seen as part of the local public sphere. This is an imagination that the craft beer movement will see itself as reviving. Even before prohibition, beer began to consolidate and as the number of breweries in one region declined, we began to see the development of a regional identity as beer became branded as part of the regional culture. Certain regions became known as beer-producing areas. As the consolidation trend continued, several brands began to emerge as national brands. Brands like Anheuser-Busch, Pabst, Schlitz, Ballantine, and others became synonymous with the national culture. As Stack (2003) points out, the development of canning also helped this national beer culture develop. Before prohibition, most beer was sold in bars and pubs. But as canning and storage developed, the purchase of canned beer increased and allowed the national breweries to dramatically increase their market share. The national beer culture was associated with American leisure, the postwar culture of consumption, and particular large brands.

## Authenticity

We talked about community and authenticity in Chapter 1. But we will briefly discuss those two concepts again in order to think about the historical development of craft beer.

Authenticity is an important theme for the craft beer movement that has grown out of an imagination of the history of beer. Authenticity plays differently at different historical moments and in different regions and in different countries. And the notion of authenticity is a contradictory one. A general theme is that big beer is not interesting or even good. The beer critic Michael Jackson once said that it was interesting that Budweiser goes through a lot of trouble to make a very light in flavor beer.[1] A general theme in the craft beer culture is that national beer had watered down its product to reach a larger mass audience. The postwar consumer culture of mass consumption had undermined the quality of beer. Light beer is a clear example of this critique. Further, for many years in the craft beer movement, this assumption of mediocrity was also associated with lager. While the first generation of craft beer producers brewed mostly lagers, it took a while for lagers to catch on as a desirable commodity within the later movement. Adjunct lagers, which were the mainstay of the big brewers, were seen as watered down, bland beer made for mass consumption. This beer was seen as inauthentic, and so lager became associated with the idea of inauthenticity.

Because light beers and adjunct lagers were produced with corn sugar and other sugar adjuncts, these adjuncts were seen as inauthentic, and originally were not considered appropriate for craft beer. True beer style became an important part of the drive for authenticity. The craft community opened itself to the exploration of different styles of beer from different European countries primarily. And so Belgian ales, English ales, and German ales became highly valued. It was really the consumers of craft beer who would see lager as synonymous with adjunct lagers and light beer. And the market was driven toward ale. It is also true that ales are easier to produce, and easier to influence their flavor, creating more space for creativity. It would be a while before the craft community returned to valuing lagers, and when it did, there was an exploration of lagers from Schwarzbier, to Gose to Altbier and more. To this day, there are still discussions on lists like BeerAdvocate asking, "why do people think lagers suck?"

Further, American craft brewers felt free to experiment with these different styles of beer and create genuinely American variations of the different styles. This opened a very interesting tension in craft beer that continues to this day. Beers are judged in competitions at both the professional and amateur level on how well they demonstrate the style. And so, there are beer style guidelines like the Beer Judge Certification Program (BJCP) Style Guidelines. These guidelines form the basis for how beers are categorized so that they can be judged at competitions. And for beer makers, competitions are very important. For craft brewers, they indicate that one is an excellent craftsperson. But just as important to being a good craftsperson, winning a competition is really good for marketing your quality up-market beer. At the same time, brewers in America are constantly pushing the boundaries of style and so brewers create India Pale Lagers, New England IPAs, etc. These new styles then have to be incorporated into the style guidelines if they catch on and become an important part of the culture and the market.

Probably the most important element of the drive for authenticity was the ideology of craft and the craftsperson. Craft involves a focus on quality, the craftsperson is held to a higher standard, craft is a calling. This ideology not only helps craft beer define itself, but it comes out of a history of defining itself against "big beer." While brewers must sell their beer and they are concerned about the market, the drive is for excellence. This is one of the psychological reasons that competitions and awards are important. The brewers in an area themselves have ideas about who are the best brewers in the community, and they are admired. This emphasis on quality and craft produced another tension in the craft beer culture. From the early days of craft brewing, one of the definitions of a craft brewery was how big (or really how small it was). The Brewers Association, the main trade association for craft beer, defines craft production as producing 6 million barrels of beer (or less) annually. They emphasize that the brewery is independent and focused on quality. Of course, 6 million barrels is a lot of beer. This number has expanded over the years to continue to include some of the largest craft breweries in the definition. So size is a definite tension. There is also a concern in the community about hype. While America may be the land of inventiveness and the creation of new styles, there is also a concern for gimmick versus a genuine invention of a creative new style.

## Community

Closely linked to an imagination of authenticity, ideas about craft and craftspeople, as well as the broader imagination of what beer is and where it can go, is an imagination of community. We will see the theme of community coming up throughout the book. From the beginning, craft beer producers and consumers saw themselves as a community that stood in opposition to mainstream mass consumption of "big beer." There are many variations on this community theme. Part of the theme is about defining, originally by size, as to what a craft brewery was. The Brewer's Association definition of a craft brewer, taken from their website is:

> An American craft brewer is a small and independent brewer.
>
> **Small**
>
> Annual production of 6 million barrels of beer or less (approximately 3 percent of U.S. annual sales). Beer production is attributed to a brewer according to rules of alternating proprietorships.
>
> **Independent**
>
> Less than 25 percent of the craft brewery is owned or controlled (or equivalent economic interest) by a beverage alcohol industry member that is not itself a craft brewer.[2]

Small and independent not only defines craft brewers, but it defines a community of beer producers who stood apart from the history of beer post-WWII, which was to get larger, produce a more palatable product for the masses and be separated from local communities. And while other countries did not experience prohibition, we see the same path of the consolidation of big beer into national and later international conglomerates. As craft brewers are small and independent, they are also embedded in local communities, this is still true to this day. And as craft beer expands, this is also a tension. Some craft brewers and breweries commit to remaining local, but others seek a more national or larger regional marketplace.

## Brewing in the United States

### *Early Beer History*

For the most part, we are interested in this history of beer after WWII with the rise of the mass market for beer and national breweries. However, we can say a few words about the early history of beer in the United States. While brewing began almost as soon as Europeans arrived in North America, beer production was small and very local. Individuals brewed beer in their own homes. Pubs brewed small batches of beer stored in wooden kegs and served in the pub. It's not until the 19th century that brewing began to take off. After the Civil War, brewing became a significant industry and by 1870 there were the largest number of breweries in the United States until around 2015 when we surpassed that number. From the late 19th century to the early 20th century, electric refrigeration was invented, pasteurization became possible giving beer a longer shelf life. With immigrants from Germany and other parts of central Europe, along with the new technologies, lager brewing became possible and there was high demand for it. It is at this point that lager begins to be synonymous with mass-produced beer. By the end of the 19th century, the first national breweries began to emerge, the largest of which was Anheuser-Busch (Stack, 2003).

In the United States, it's not possible to talk about the history of craft beer, or beer in general, without talking about prohibition. Immediately before prohibition, there were over 1300 breweries in the United States. Earlier, in 1870 there were over 3200 breweries, so consolidation began before prohibition. By the time prohibition ended, there were around 750 breweries remaining. And while the numbers started to pick up in the following years, we only recently passed the number of breweries that existed in 1870. This, of course, greatly helped the corporate consolidation of breweries into what has now come to be thought of as "big beer." Prohibition was not the only thing that allowed for the development of big beer. In every regional beer market, there are specific stories about breweries merging, going out of business, or selling to larger breweries. Prohibition not only left a few large breweries standing, but it also left a space for shipped beer to develop. Before prohibition, most beer was consumed in bars at the tap. But with many breweries going out of business, and the development of canned beer, it became possible to ship more beer to more places. This began before WWII but after WWII canning, better techniques for beer preservation, refrigeration in the home, and a desire for mass-produced products allowed a few national breweries to come to dominate beer production. This beer was lager beer that became synonymous with beer. The locus of consumption shifted during this time too. While earlier generations drank beer in bars and local pubs, after WWII beer was primarily consumed in the home.

Pennsylvania with its large German population was one of the states, along with New York, that had the greatest number of breweries in the mid-19th century. At the same time, there were several hundred breweries in Philadelphia. The breweries were very much neighborhood breweries and served the people in specific parts of the city. After prohibition, 17 breweries came back to Philadelphia to face a number of challenges to resume business (Wagner, 2012). This book is not concerned with the specific story of the fate of those breweries, but like many cities the numbers went down to one or two and by the 1980s there were no breweries left in Philadelphia (Wagner, 2012). The Philadelphia market then was primarily a market for the consumption of national brands and this consumption was primarily in the home in bottles or cans. It is not until the beginning of craft beer that we see breweries begin to emerge again in Philadelphia.

### *Postwar Mass Culture and Mass Culture Beer*

After WWII, we saw the development of a mass consumer culture in the United States, Europe, Asia, and other industrialized nations. From the early days of capitalism, consumption has been an important part of development. One can think of the rise of modern advertising and companies like J. Walter Thompson developed new skills linking products to images and images to desirable settings as the early steps in the development of technologies of consumption. But as the 20th century moves on, national media, first magazines and newspapers, then radio and TV, become the means by which the new technologies of consumption are deployed (Ewen & Ewen, 1982; Ohmann, 1987; Poster, 2001). We can see refrigeration, preserving, canning, and trucking of beer as another set of technologies of consumption. And while these inventions were not designed for the beer market, they are taken up by successful beer producers as a means of increasing production and sales. These technologies of mass producing and distributing beer also needed the postwar semiotic systems of advertising and marketing these products to a mass audience.

By necessity then, beer started to become very standardized nationally. To appeal to the mass market, producers had to reach for the least common denominator. Lager had already, in the late 19th century, become the preferred style. And lager lent itself to mass production and consumption.

It was clear and crisp and tasted very good cold. Further, the hop content could be reduced and adjunct sugars like corn and rice could be used to further smooth the beer. This led to a lager that was bland, in a certain sense, because the breweries were looking not to offend any portion of the beer drinking market. Further, the differences between different brands were subtle, as all producers were engaged in a similar process. This is not unlike other mass-produced products that were aimed at a standardized product that could be sold to a mass market. The common denominator became a theme of postwar consumer society. It is also one of the things that people criticized in this market, people had access to lots of things, none of which were at all distinctive. Malvina Reynolds song *Little Boxes* is a nice critique of the postwar consumer society.

Interestingly, while a similar massification and corporate concentration process of beer production and consumption was going on in Europe in countries like Denmark and Germany, the lagers produced in these counties were still hoppier in flavor and had a stronger taste overall. This is perhaps due to the longer brewing history in these countries that was not interrupted by prohibition. In England and Belgium, the tradition was to produce more ales and not as many lagers. In England, the concentration of production leading to large producers like Greene King happened through a different route that involved the buying of cellars, taps, and pubs. Today many English breweries are owned by foreign companies or investors. We'll talk more about British history below.

## Craft Beer Begins in the United States

The massification of food and beverages in the United States and other countries continues to this day. Studies show the increased consumption of sugar, soda, fat, salt, fast food, etc. And at the same time, there is the parallel development of upmarket tastes in food and beverages. The slow food movement, the rise of farmers' markets, organic food, and veganism are all signs of the movement of taste, as well as the proliferation of taste communities. Coffee and wine have gone from mass market products for most people to exclusive specialized products grown on small estates and produced in specialty coffee houses and local wineries. Beer experienced a similar revolution. Some of our informants talked about growing up in a world of bland national beer and seeking other tastes. These entrepreneurs initially perceived this as a disharmony, beer was lacking in flavor that somehow it should have (Spinosa, Flores & Dreyfus, 1997). And this generation (or generations) turned to Europe and countries like Germany, Belgium, and England for other styles of beer and other tastes. It is not surprising that when Jim Koch first began advertising Sam Adams beer, his attack was not American big beer, but rather the larger producers of imported beer. Import beer was the "quality" flavor that Koch was arguing Sam Adams was better than (Hindy, 2014).

Craft beer, then, has a very specific history. But it is also part of a set of cultural changes around social class, taste, and the fragmentation of the mass market of the postwar into smaller, more specialized taste markets. As mentioned above, this fragmentation was felt in other food and beverage markets as well. California cuisine is perhaps a good example of this taste revolution. The west coast chefs focused on local produce, quality, and lighter faire. This began as a regional California cuisine, but over time became a national phenomenon. What we today largely think of as farm to table began in California in the 1960s and 1970s. At the same time, fast food experienced exponential growth and certainly was a much bigger movement than the farm to table movement with its focus on local and quality ingredients. Simultaneously, many of the smaller wineries were starting up in California and other parts of the west coast. And while the bigger wineries were focused on mass production and big taste, many of the smaller wineries looked to France for their inspiration and sought to make a local quality product.

This fragmentation or segmentation of the food and beverage market is also about the continued evolution of consumer capitalism at the end of the 20th and beginning of the 21st century. Market segmentations, target marketing, the proliferation of products have affected all consumer industries, and craft beer is part of this shifting landscape. In fact, craft beer is an interesting example, as it begins while most of the beer market is still focused on the mass-produced, uniform product, from producers like Anheuser-Busch and Miller Coors. Those early craft breweries really suffered to find an audience and many struggled to stay open. It could be said that the founders of these craft breweries were on the cutting edge of the same taste movement that was going on with cuisine, coffee, and wine, but there was not much of an audience yet for the product.

As the decades moved from the 1980s to the 2000s, markets and tastes shifted, and craft brewers found themselves with a large and growing market. We could think of from about 2010 to 2015 being a "golden age" but good growth in sales began before that. In Chapter 2, we showed a graph of craft beer production and the growth of production. Figure 3.1 is a graph of the craft brewery growth by different categories.

As there are now many more breweries and different kinds of breweries, several of the authors on books about craft beer think about this historical movement through the idea of generations (Acitelli, 2013; Hindy, 2014). The generational model is not the only way to think about the history of craft beer. But it is useful for thinking about how people see craft beer, and why some breweries are successful. It is also useful for thinking about different geographic regions and when the movement began in their area. The first generation in one location might jump into the industry when the larger industry is up to generation 3. That will affect what the new brewery in the location that developed later will do and become. Below we will pursue this notion of generations of craft brewers to think about the history of craft beer.

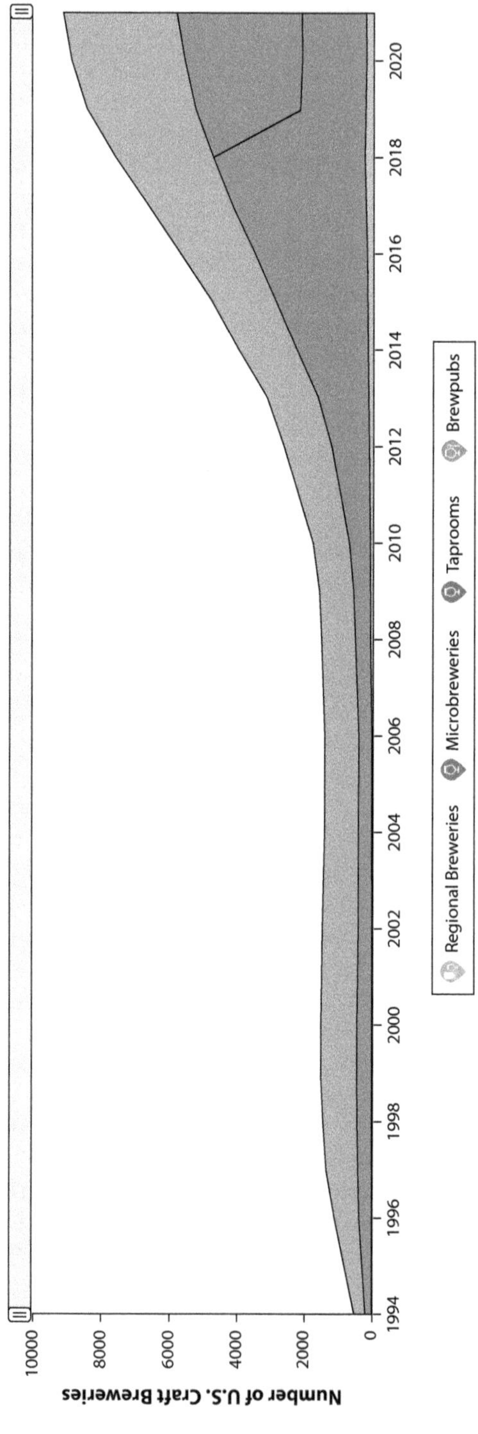


*Figure 3.1* U.S. Craft Brewery Count by Category

Source: © Brewers Association.

### *Generations*

Hindy (2014), in his excellent insider history of the craft beer movement, uses a notion of generations to define the unfolding of the craft beer movement. Hindy was a co-founder of Brooklyn Brewing, one of the early craft beer breweries in New York and so was very well situated to discuss the history of the movement including the struggles in the industry that he personally participated in. For Hindy, he talks mostly about Generation 0, Generation 1, and Generation 2. He refers to generation 0 as the pioneers, the people who began independent small breweries before craft was a thing. A key person at this stage is Fritz Maytag, who bought Anchor Brewing and who many consider the grandfather of the craft beer movement. Maytag's interest in Anchor began because he frequented a restaurant in San Francisco that served Anchor beer. At the time Maytag began to look at Anchor's business, they were on a path to going out of business. They were victims of the growing national market for mass-produced lighter beers. Maytag first bought a controlling interest in Anchor in 1965, and then eventually bought out the company. His goal was to keep producing Anchor steam beer. While he wanted the company to be successful, he was committed to Anchor remaining small and local. They were mostly supplying beer to the restaurants and bars in and around San Francisco. Anchor did not begin to bottle Anchor beer until the 1970s.

At the same time, Maytag was working to ensure that Anchor would survive, Jack McAuliffe was in the navy and assigned to work in Scotland. He experienced Scottish beers and began to brew while in Scotland. He bought a copy of Dave Line's *The Big Book of Brewing* to educate himself in the practice of homebrewing. In the UK, homebrewing was legal but still a very new hobby. Not many people were doing it and Line was a very early source for how to brew beer. McAuliffe returned to the United States, continued to homebrew and in 1976 founded New Albion Brewing. This is one of the first microbreweries in the United States. McAuliffe was a very important generation 0 figure as he influenced the first generation of craft brewers like Jim Koch and homebrewers like Charlie Papazian (Acitelli, 2013; Hindy, 2014).

Papazian will go on to organize a homebrewing classes in Boulder where he had moved to be a teacher. Some of the enthusiastic homebrewers will go on to become craft brewers. He founded the American Homebrewing Association in 1978 as well as other organizations. In 1984, he published *The Complete Joy of Homebrewing*, which has since become the bible for many generations of homebrewers (Papazian, 1984). And since homebrewing is where most craft brewers got their start, this book was incredibly important to craft beer.

McAuliffe emphasized New Albion's beer was made with pure ingredients with no adjuncts. So, the goal was to separate the beer from New Albion, a locally crafted product, from the highly processed national scale beers that had become in the postwar the model for what beer was. McAuliffe had two other partners and they put together a very small-scale brewery in a warehouse in California outside of San Francisco. While McAuliffe was a very interesting brewer, they could not find an investor to support the growth and development of the brewery. Craft beer was not yet an everyday concept that consumers or investors understood. And so, the brewery did not last very long.

Redhook brewery, in Seattle, is another interesting story about breweries in these early days. Redhook was founded in 1981 by Paul Shipman, a wine merchant, and Gordon Bowker, the co-founder of Starbucks. Redhook's founders were better funded than McAuliffe at New Albion. They bought a German brewing system and hired a brewmaster. Rather than going with established yeast laboratories, they went with a yeast developed at the University of Washington. The first beer they produced had a lot of esters that were similar to Belgian beers and so the beer had flavors that were considered off flavors of banana and clove. In Seattle, many customers wondered what was wrong with the beer and the rumor that the brewery was infected began to spread. The beer critic Michael Jackson, who we mentioned above came to visit the brewery and praised the beer for its Belgian characteristics. Jackson had quickly become the spokesperson for craft beer and for its aesthetic qualities. So, his endorsement was important. But at the same time, it did not change the public's mind whose tastes were not yet ready for the fruity Belgian style ales. Eventually, Redhook changed its yeast and began to produce an IPA that was more in line with what craft beer consumers were considering beer at the time.

While Redhook's story is not a story of an early brewery failure, it illustrates the constraints that many of the early craft breweries were dealing with. On the one hand, there was a movement to produce beers that were more local and did not contain a lot of added ingredients. And there was an interest in new flavors, and as Michael Jackson said at the time, more flavorful beers. On the other hand, most Americans had not experienced beers with a wide flavor profile. Most Americans were familiar with German lager styles and specifically pilsner style lighter beers. Some Americans had begun to branch out to taste English ales, although in bottles and chilled to American tastes. Belgian beers with fruity esters were largely unknown to the American palate, it would be another decade or so before a consuming public would seek such flavors.

Hindy (2014) sees the first generation of craft brewers existing from around 1984 to 1994. This first generation caught the excitement of brewers who were interested in craft beer and the development of craft beer. But like generation 0, there was not yet a large market for craft beer. So many of the breweries in generation 0 struggled financially to keep their operations going. Another thing to add about the early breweries, many craft brewers used contract brewers to produce their beers and begin to create their brand. Getting the startup capital to create a brewery was very difficult as we saw in the New Albion case. It was easier to have a recipe and contract with large breweries to produce the beer. This is how Jim Koch started with Boston Beer Company. Samuel Adams Boston Lager was a recipe that Koch had brewed by contract with the Pittsburgh Brewing Company. It allowed him to get up to production very quickly without investing a lot of money in the kettles and tanks that would be needed for a brewery. Early on, many of the craft brewers did not like Koch. Jim Koch was really more of a businessman and less of a brewer. He was skilled at marketing and promotion and moved Sam Adams very quickly into a popular spot with the American public that it enjoys to this day. Over the longer haul, Jim Koch was good for the craft-brewing community, but in the early days there was a lot of tension.

Pete's Brewing Company that produced Pete's Wicked Ale was also contract brewed and was one of the early big craft beers. Like Jim Koch, Pete Slosberg was also very skilled at advertising and marketing. Pete's Wicked Ale was a beer, like Sam Adams, that the public came to know and represented for much of the buying public what the new craft beer movement was. Pete's was so successful that it became a multimillion-dollar operation and went to a public offering. The company that bought Pete's did not use the skillful ad strategies that had made such a big brand, and through benign neglect, the brand finally was closed in 2012 (Hindy, 2014).

So, contract brewing had a significant place in this first generation of craft brewing, because buying equipment, supplies and figuring out how to market and distribute your product was very daunting. Most craft breweries at the time lived on the brink of financial insolvency. This is something that forged them into a community and one that shared with each other to keep each other alive. That's why many of the early craft brewers did not like Jim Koch. But it is also how the community norms and the ideals of craft beer as small, independent, and community oriented developed. Craft became a culture and an ideology as much as it was a movement in taste and beverage production. Up until 2008, contract brewing was still a growing segment of the craft market, although it did not grow as fast as regional breweries did in the early 2000s. After 2008, contract brewing really became a very small segment of the craft beer market.

Hindy (2014) defines Generation 2 as between the years of 1994 and 2000. Several things mark this generation. First is the growing success of craft beer. There is now beginning to be a sizable market for craft beer. Hindy states that the industry grew by 50% between 1994 and 1995. And while there are some ups and downs in the growth of the industry, craft beer will begin a period of continued growth that will go until 2019. From 2012 to 2015, the period of most of our data collection, the growth of the industry was dramatic. This meant that many in the second generation of craft brewing experienced dramatic success and have become some of the biggest craft breweries. He further points out that many of the first generation of craft brewers are still focused on lager beers and the ideas coming from the German purity laws that beer is just malt, water, yeast, and hops. But in the second generation, brewers begin to explore other styles, other traditions, and begin to experiment with other additives in beer. The first two examples of generation 2 that we will mention here are New Belgium in Colorado and Allagash Brewing in Maine. Both breweries were specifically focused on developing Belgian style beers. We saw with Redhook that the public was not ready to consider a fruity beer, but now this becomes more possible.

New Belgium Brewing was founded by Jeff Lebesch and Kim Jordan in 1991. Lebesch was a homebrewer in Fort Collins, Colorado and was familiar with making English and German style beers. In 1988, he went on a bike tour in Belgium and traveled to numerous breweries sampling Belgian style beers and taking notes on what he found. Lebesch said that the Belgian beers opened his eyes to the range of tastes that could be possible with beer (Laxen, 2018). Lebesch and Jordan, who were romantic partners as well as business partners, began a small brewery in the home cobbling together brewing equipment from old dairy equipment. While Lebesch oversaw brewing, Jordan was doing all aspects of the business from keeping the books to managing beer delivery in the Fort Collins area. While the era of readily available brewing equipment had not yet arrived for craft brewers, tastes had begun to change. One of Lebesch's first beers was a Belgian amber that would become Fat Tire. Lebesch said in an interview, that one of the breakthroughs in brewing a Belgian beer is when they used the yeast dregs from a bottle of Belgian beer. It was at that point that he realized that it was the Belgian yeast that gave Belgian beers the complex flavors that they have (Laxen, 2018). Fat Tire immediately became very popular such that they realized they could not brew enough with their current equipment and the expansion of New Belgium really began at this point. In 2018, New Belgium was the fourth largest craft brewery in the United States.

Coming from a progressive tradition in the Fort Collins area, New Belgium has always been concerned with environmental causes, remaining connected to the local community and as Jordan said in an interview with Inc. magazine, making sure that the value that was produced by the brewery was shared with the workers in the brewery (Winfrey, 2020). In the same article, Jordan discusses a fact that is well known in the brewing community. In 2012, after becoming sole owner of New Belgium, Jordan sold the company to the employees of New Belgium. This is one of the most powerful demonstrations of the values of craft finding themselves somewhere beyond the idea of an entrepreneurial founder only being concerned with the wealth that is produced by a new venture. At the same time, New Belgium became so big that being managed locally was perhaps too much and Jordan negotiated a sale for the employee-owned company to Lion Little World Beverages, a subsidiary of Kirin. This pressure of success, and the pressure to be concerned for the management of capital is something we will talk about later in the book.

Two examples of generation 2 breweries coming from the West Coast are Stone Brewing and Russian River Brewing. There are a number of West Coast breweries that could be discussed here in generation 2, but Stone and Russian

River were central to the establishment of the West Coast IPA style. With its very strong use of bittering and flavoring hops, rich malt and higher alcohol content, the West Coast IPA became a very popular beer and perhaps one of the first truly American style beers. It certainly played a role in the establishment of national IPA day that is celebrated on the first Thursday in August. While the hype around national IPA day has died down, it was a strong media event in 2011 when it was established and for several years after that. And while Hindy (2014) would see Stone and Russian River as part of the second generation of craft, Acitelli (2013, p. 302) suggests that Vinnie Cilurzo and his wife Natalie, owners of Russian River Brewing, were part of "…the craft beer movement's fourth wave." The difference in the dating could be explained by the focus on the industry versus the individuals. While Hindy is thinking about how the industry evolved from a pre-generation to a first, second, and third generation with different market and structural conditions, Acitelli is talking about the individual brewers and what creative beers would have already existed in their world. He suggests that Cilurzo, as well as Greg Koch (no relation to Jim Koch founder of Boston Beer Company) and Steve Wagner, founders of Stone Brewing, would have already known Anchor Steam Beer, and Sierra Nevada Pale Ale as beers that were part of the normal beer market. This would not have been true for earlier generations.

Wagner and Koch met at a UC-Davis extension course on beer (Acitelli, 2013, p. 257). Both were musicians, Koch had gotten very interested in craft beer living in the Los Angeles area. Wagner was a homebrewer in the San Francisco area. They became friends and began to talk about finding a place to open a brewery, they finally settled on an area north of San Diego, very near the area that Vinne Cilurzo was from. This was a time of a lot of growth in the craft beer movement in California. Stone began brewing in 1996 and by 1997 had a couple of beers they were producing. Several of Stone's IPAs, including Arrogant Bastard, would come to help define the West Coast IPA. Central to the style was a strong bitter flavor created by adding a significant amount of bittering hops. The bitterness was balanced by a sweeter caramel malt, reminiscent of British IPAs.

Vinnie Cilurzo was a homebrewer who began Blind Pig Brewery in Temecula, California, north of San Diego in 1994. It was the only craft brewery in the area for a few years. Greg Koch met Vinnie when he stopped in Blind Pig when looking for a location in the San Diego area for Stone Brewing. They would get to know each other well. Blind Pig became locally famous with Blind Pig IPA, one of the early West Coast IPAs. Cilurzo would become something of a star in the craft beer community. Cilurzo would leave Blind Pig to become head brewer for Russian River Brewing in Santa Rosa, CA, north of San Francisco. Russian River was owned by Korbel Champagne Cellars. Korbel sold Russian River to Cilurzo and his wife in 2002. Russian River would go on to produce some of the most famous beers including Pliny the Elder and Pliny the Younger. Cilurzo also began to explore Belgian styles, wild yeast fermentation, and barrel aging.

There are many other brewers and breweries we could discuss that form this second generation of craft brewing. But there are other books that do a great job with this history (Acitelli,2013; Hindy, 2014). So, we will move on to talk about what comes next.

While the internet became a feature of life in the 1980s, it is not until the 1990s and beyond that it is a regular part of people's daily lives. One of our theses in this book is that the internet and then social media was central to the growth of the craft beer movement especially during this second generation and after. The internet allowed for the sharing of productive capacity. Brewers were able to buy used equipment, share with others in the brewing community about their problems and their needs. One of our informants explained that in the early days (for him) brewers borrowed yeast from each other, shared problems, etc., because they had to. By 2016, this was no longer such an important need. Probably most importantly, breweries used the internet, and later social media to advertise and to build hype. An important part of the craft beer community are the new beer releases, the special craft beer events, etc. One popular brewery in the Philadelphia area would post on social media about a new bottle release. Immediately, the following days there would be long lines of fans lining up to get some of the new release. We will talk more about social media in Chapter 6.

Hindy (2014) places the third generation of craft breweries as those that came about post-2000. He suggests that at that point there are several different paths. Some breweries decide to be small and fit within an existing ecosystem of craft beer. This is certainly a common theme among breweries that come about in big cities that are already dominated by several successful craft breweries. But of course, there are other areas in the United States and the world where craft beer had not yet become a popular commodity. In these areas, some ventured in with large capital backing and began with a large-scale brewery. 3 Daughters Brewing in St. Petersburg, FL, is a good example of this strategy. St. Pete is a city where the excitement around craft beer started a little later. 3 Daughters was founded by a pair of restaurateurs who wanted to make beer for their business. As they saw the market grow, they jumped right into a large 30-barrel brewing system. The business began in 2013. Another example is Mikkeller, a brewing company in Denmark, founded by two friends who were inspired by the craft beer movement in the United States and began to brew unique beers and win competitions. The company was founded in 2006, and started out originally as a gypsy brewery, but eventually began their own brewing. Gypsy brewers were people with unique brewing skills and interesting recipes. They brewed their beers at different breweries and did not have a location of their own. In the 2000s into the 2010s, gypsy breweries were seen as artistic and cool. It was the maverick artist popping onto the scene. Today that excitement has died down. Mikkeller has not only been central to the craft beer movement in Denmark, but they have also established collaborations with breweries in the United States creating a connection between the beer scenes in the two countries. So, in Hindy's third generation, a lot of different things were going on.

## Craft Brewing in Philadelphia

One of our informants in the Philadelphia area also used a generational model to discuss craft beer in the larger Philadelphia metropolitan area similar to Hindy's generational model. Our informant began with the 1994 generation and called that generation 1. While there were earlier craft breweries in the Philadelphia area that paralleled the early days of craft beer in other places, the 1990s generation was the beginning of large successful craft breweries in the area, so it is not surprising that the informant saw the 1990s generation as the first generation. Those breweries include Yards Brewing, Philadelphia Brewing Company, Flying Fish Brewing, Dogfish Head Brewing, Victory Brewing, and Iron Hill Brewing. Except for Iron Hill, which committed to being a series of brewpubs, these breweries are the largest ones in the Philadelphia area.

Our informant not only has a generational model, but it is also an ecological model too. From the informant's perspective, these large breweries took up the entire ecological zone for large craft breweries. What was left was space for the smaller microbreweries. This in the informant's model would be the second generation for the Philadelphia area. There are many breweries in the generation but perhaps a good example would be Conshohocken Brewing that opened in 2014 with a 15-barrel system. This size is typical of microbreweries and larger brewpubs. After this second generation, our informant saw the coming of nanobreweries and very small businesses beginning perhaps around 2018. The informant did not think this ecological level would be sustainable as it would not produce enough money for business to survive over a longer period. While we think our informant is right about the ecological model, we have also seen a regional proliferation of breweries and brewpubs. Earlier, when there were fewer breweries in the Philadelphia area, it made sense to see the whole metropolitan area as part of the Philly beer scene. And indeed, many still see breweries this way. But as the economy has developed, many areas have their own brewing culture, and so the Philadelphia craft beer community now looks more rhizomatic, a series of overlapping smaller circles perhaps, rather than one large region one can draw a circle around.

There was an earlier generation in the craft brewing scene in Philadelphia in the way that Hindy would define it. The brewpubs included Dock Street Brewing, Sam Adams Brew House, and Manayunk Brewery and Restaurant. The production breweries included Yards Brewing, Independence Brewing, Gravity Brewing, and Red Bell Brewing. All the production breweries began in the late 1980s and 1990s. Like a lot of breweries at that time, they often began using a contract brewery, or at some points relying on a contract brewery to brew for them. The Sam Adams Brewhouse is an interesting story. David Mink, owner of the Sansom Street Oyster house, a very popular restaurant in Philadelphia, was interested in bringing brewing back to Philadelphia. He made a deal with Jim Koch, owner of Boston Beer Company to start a brewpub on the second floor above the Oyster House. Koch supplied the recipes, and the beers were brewed on site in a small brewery (Wagner, 2012). In 1989, laws in Pennsylvania had changed to legalize brewpubs providing they sold onsite in the brewery's own pub (Wagner, 2012). Mink later closed Sam Adams and opened a popular craft beer bar in the newly fashionable Northern Liberties section of Philadelphia called Standard Tap. In terms of the production breweries, they all struggled given that this was still early days for craft brewing and a culture of consumers had not yet been built up. By the early 2000s, Yards was the only production brewery left within the city limits (Wagner, 2012).

Generation 2, in Hindy's sense, (generation 1 in our informant's model) includes Yards Brewing (1994), Philadelphia Brewing Company (2007), Flying Fish (1995), Dogfish Head (1995), Victory Brewing (1996), and Iron Hill (1996). All these breweries, except Iron Hill, began as production breweries, and while they each have pubs in the brewery, the primary focus of the brewery was the production of beer for bottle and keg distribution. By now, some of these breweries are producing large quantities of craft beer and their bottles and cans are available in multiple states. As we can see, in their second generation, there is a pattern, but there are exceptions. Philadelphia Brewing Company (PBC) started in 2007, which is more of a generation 3 time period. We include PBC in generation 2 because they came about from a split within Yards Brewing Company. After disagreements about future directions, co-owners William Barton, Nancy Barton, and Tom Kehoe agreed to split the company. The Bartons retained the brewery location for Yards as well as the equipment. They went on to design new beers and become PBC. Kehoe retained the recipes for Yards beers as well as the Yards name. Kehoe went on to establish a new brewery location after contract brewing for a few years (Wagner, 2012). So really PBC is part of the 1990s movement.

The other more unusual story is Iron Hill where the founders set out from the beginning to create a brew pub and the restaurant was as important as the brewery. Thus, the brewery at Iron Hill remained smaller than the other breweries. We include Iron Hill in generation 2 because it started in the 1990s and was part of the craft beer community of that time. Further, Iron Hill has been a very winning brewery at craft beer competitions, many of their beers have won awards. Finally, Iron Hill created, almost from the beginning an expansion model with a chain of Iron Hill brew pubs. Their current goal is to open 20 brewpubs and in 2020 they opened a larger production brewery. One final important thing about Iron Hill is that the brewpub model has become something of a growth model for some of the smaller production breweries in the third generation.

Generation 3 in Hindy's sense begins in the early 2000s and perhaps continues to the present. While one could imagine a fourth generation, from a structural sense it makes sense to consider the current moment still part of the third generation. The third generation includes more small production breweries and important brewpubs. As examples, our model of the smaller production breweries are Conshohocken Brewing, Neshaminy Creek Brewing, and Attic Brewing. Two very important brewpubs would be Tired Hands and Forest and Main. Conshohocken Brewing was opened in 2014 on the bike path in Conshohocken. Their logo is a person on a traditional penny-farthing high wheeler bike. Any day on the Schuylkill River Trail bike path one will see dozens of bikes in the bike racks and bikers hanging out on the porch of the brewery or just inside where the garage door windows are open sipping a pint after a nice ride. Conshohocken started out as a smaller brewery, but it was very popular with the bike community and people in the local neighborhood. It was a good model of how a production brewery could work on a smaller scale. In our interview with the head brewer, he told us that about 50% of the production by volume was sold out of the pub attached to the brewery. So, the little pub on the bike path was very important to Conshohocken Brewing's success.

More recently, Conshohocken has opened a series of pubs and brewpubs as well as an additional production facility. So, their expansion has really been hybrid. Not just one big production facility or just a chain of brewpubs, but rather a combination of different kinds of sites. They now have five locations. More breweries have been like this. Neshaminy Creek Brewing opened in 2010 north of the city. They have had a reputation of being a very creative brewery and for a small brewery have one several important awards. In 2022, they again won a gold award for their Mexican lager at the World Cup of Beer. For a small production brewery, Neshaminy Creek has a very large reputation in the Philadelphia area. Similar to Conshohocken Brewing, they have opened two satellite locations. Finally in our sample of small-production breweries, we can also mention Attic Brewing. Attic was part of our homebrew community, and they opened in the Germantown neighborhood of Philadelphia. Attic opened in December 2019 and then had to almost immediately close the taproom and switch to canning because of the pandemic. Attic is in a mostly black neighborhood in Philadelphia, and while the owners are white, many of the employees at Attic are black. Further, one thing that stands out about Attic is its very progressive attitude toward people with different gender identities and people of color. While on any given day the clients might be mostly white, there are more people of color at Attic than one sees at most other craft beer bars. Attic was very innovative as well. Now their tap room is back open, but during the pandemic they developed an outdoor seating operation. They also began to deliver canned beer throughout the Philadelphia area. This strategy probably kept them going during the worst of the pandemic.

As mentioned above, a couple of iconic brewpubs in generation 3 would include Tired Hands and Forest & Main. Both brewpubs are very different, but their difference shows some of the range among brewpubs. And in the last few years, there are many brewpubs that have cropped up in the Philadelphia area. At the time that Forest & Main, and Tired Hands opened up, people could list the outstanding brewpubs of the Philadelphia area. But now there are too many to list. They really are becoming, once again, the neighborhood pub. Forest & Main was founded by two brewers, one who had apprenticed in another brewery and focused on Belgian ales. The other brewer was trained in the UK and did British style ales. Forest & Main became very well known in the Philadelphia area for their high-quality and authentic British and Belgian style beers. But they were also very experimental and cultivated local wild yeasts to make more sour and funky tasting beers. Located in a large Victorian House just off the main street in Ambler, PA, Forest & Main was also a very good restaurant, and it was really the closest thing to a very good English pub in the Philadelphia area. One could get a beautifully crafted dinner and an extraordinary pint to go with it. From the early days of Forest & Main, they had planned to find a location for a larger brewery as they were brewing constantly at capacity. The pandemic not only pushed that plan but changed their orientation. They moved to a larger space on the main street with a larger brewery. They have maintained on onsite pub, but they no longer have the restaurant. They, like a lot of small breweries, have also moved to canning and selling beers from their storefront.

Tired hands is a similar but also different story. The brewpub began as a very small store front in the town of Ardmore. Originally there was a brewing team and a bread-making team. One could get fresh bread, some simple snacks and beer. Tired Hands beer was unique. There were lots of unique sour beers, and more unusual grain bills. Craft beer fans flocked to Tired Hands because there were so many interesting and different beers. While the beers were brewed in small batch, there were a few house regular beers and then a number of rotating specialty beers, it was really beer as an art form. In 2015, they opened the Fermentaria, it was a larger brewery with a capacity for around 10,000 barrels per year and a larger restaurant. Diners would get to sit among the oak barrels for aging and souring beer with the larger brewery equipment in the background. A unique space.

As we said above, there are many more breweries and brewpubs in Philadelphia that we could discuss. This is true in many cities. At the current moment, big breweries are getting bigger, new brewpubs are opening, but growth of beer sales is slowing. The COVID-19 pandemic put a real crimp in craft beer sales, but even before the pandemic, growth was slowing. In the last year or so (2021–22), craft beer sales by volume have almost recovered. But it does not look like the market will have the big growth that it experienced from 2010 to 2015. We think that perhaps the "golden era" of craft beer may be behind us, and we may be looking at a structure of the industry that looks like the wine industry with several very large wineries dominating sales, and then lots of smaller wineries that cater to local audiences and specialize in a style profile.

## Notes

1 Interview with Terry Gross on *Fresh Air* October 27, 1993, Part 2 of a two-part interview.
2 https://www.brewersassociation.org/statistics-and-data/craft-brewer-definition/

## References

Acitelli, T. (2013). *The audacity of hops: The history of America's craft beer revolution*. Chicago, IL: Chicago Review Press.
Ewen, S., & Ewen, E. (1982). *Channels of desire: Mass images and the shaping of American consciousness*. New York, NY: McGraw-Hill Book Company.
Hindy, S. (2014). *The craft beer revolution: How a band of microbrewers is transforming the World's favorite drink*. New York, NY: Palgrave Macmillan.
Laxen, J. (2018) New Belgium founder Jeff Lebesch shares insights on life after beer. *The Coloradoan*, March 22. https://www.coloradoan.com/story/life/food/beer/2018/03/22/new-belgium-founder-jeff-lebesch-shares-insights-life-after-beer/417819002/
Ohmann, R. (1987). *Politics of letters*. Middletown, CT: Wesleyan University Press.
Papazian, C. (1984). *The complete joy of homebrewing*. New York, NY: Avon Books.
Poster, M. (2001). *What's the matter with the internet?* Minneapolis, MN: University of Minnesota Press.
Spinosa, C., Flores, F., & Dreyfus, H. L. (1997). *Disclosing new worlds: Entrepreneurship, democratic action, and the cultivation of solidarity*. Cambridge, MA: MIT Press.
Stack, M. (2003). A Concise History of America's Brewing Industry. In R. Whaples (Ed.), EH.Net Encyclopedia. Retrieved July 4, 2003, from http://eh.net/encyclopedia/a-concise-history-of-americas-brewing-industry/
Wagner, R. (2012). *Philadelphia Beer: A heady history of brewing in the cradle of liberty*. Charleston, SC: The History Press.
Winfrey, G. (2020) Before selling her craft beer business to a beverage giant, she sold it to employees. *Inc Magazine*. September 2020 Issue. Retrieved from https://www.inc.com/magazine/202009/graham-winfrey/new-belgium-brewing-kim-jordan-esop-b-corp-acquisition-exit.html

# 4 Political Economy and Craft Beer

## Introduction

This chapter looks at the larger political and economic context within which craft beer developed and became a major new industry. When thinking about political economy, one has to always think about history as well. The political economic context of any moment is located within a particular flow of events. And history is always complex and unpredictable, even if there are some predictable moments. In this chapter, we look at four forces, each of which arrives on the heels of the crisis in welfare capitalism (discussed below) that perhaps began in the late 1960s but was manifest in the 1970s and resulted in the move from the welfare state to the neoliberal state in the 1980s in the United States and around the developed world. The four forces we will discuss are, the information revolution, globalization and related changes in consumer capitalism, the transformation of urban spaces, and the taste revolution in consumer culture. The information revolution is primary in that it made possible different kinds of pivoting on the part of business leaders and policy makers allowing for new avenues of accumulation and the movement beyond a stagnant economy of the late 1970s. The digital revolution not only created online avenues of consumption, but it allowed a greater personalization and fragmentation of the consumer capitalist economy that had been developing since the end of WWII. If the postwar period created the possibility of mass consumption and the rise of spaces of mass consumption (like shopping malls), then the digital revolution has led to more individualized social spaces. In the United States, the movement from mass consumption to a more fragmented landscape of multiple sites of consumption has meant different things in different places, depending on population size, urban centers, and suburban spaces. Toward the end of the chapter, we will also talk about the history and political economy of beer in Britain as a counter point to the U.S. scene.

In the urban context of Philadelphia, there has been the gentrification of neighborhoods that had once declined due to deindustrialization. In these inexpensive dilapidated spaces, new bars, breweries, restaurants, cafes, wineries, and performance spaces replace factories and light industries. Whole

DOI: 10.4324/9781003109686-4

blocks of row houses were condemned to bring in new condominiums. In this way, craft beer has been at the center of urban consumer capitalist development. The process in Philadelphia that began in the early 2000s happened in San Francisco and other cities much earlier. There are other cities where the process has started more recently. There are related processes in the smaller towns and suburban areas. So, the relationship of craft beer to capitalist production is contradictory. It has found these neoliberal consumer spaces to be conducive to growth as it has fostered an alternative imagination of what to value and what work and economic value could be. The ideas about value, and about imagined new economic possibilities in the craft beer world are central to this project. And further, the digital revolution, as we will discuss in a later chapter, has made this new imagination possible. So, while much in this chapter is about larger political economic issues, we see them as central to the development of craft beer.

## From Welfare Capitalism to Neoliberalism

In the 1970s welfare capitalism, the model for stabilizing capitalist accumulation came into crisis. Popularly described as stagflation, there were high levels of inflation as well as economic stagnation due to a glut of global production that had been accelerating in the postwar and reached a point where goods had outstripped demand. The automobile industry was a good example. Once a leading industry of national economic growth, by the 1970s demand for cars and trucks had stagnated. And at the same time, the OPEC oil embargoes contributed significantly to the inflationary pressures that were already significant in this no growth era.

Harvey (1989) referred to this period of U.S. economics as the end of Fordist-Keynesianism. Fordist policies toward paying workers more than the cost of their reproduction, coupled with Keynesian economic theory that saw the state's role as one of regulating the economy by increasing or decreasing cash flow into and out of the economy. In France, this policy of economic regulation came to be known as the regulation school of economics. A key work in this era was Aglietta's (1979) *A Theory of Capitalist Regulation: The US Experience*. Central to all these arguments was the coming out of the global great depression of the 1930s, capitalist economies around the world moved to put more money into the economy through workers' wages, the regulation of interest and other means. These forms of regulation worked to restart industrial economies after the great depression around the world and to make them more stable. While "social welfare" was smaller in the United States, and much greater in the Nordic countries, most capitalist economies participated in regulation and some forms of social welfare. This economic system also allowed for and supported the growth of the postwar consumer economy. As factories globally produced more durable and soft goods, consumers were ready to buy these products. It promoted a consumer culture of affluence and sameness. Regulation, under the dominance of the U.S. economy and the U.S. dollar, worked very well in the 1950s and 1960s. But by the end of the 1960s, this system began to stagnate. Economies around the world had modernized and were producing more goods than people were able to consume. And so, the entire "regulation" system went into crisis.

In Harvey's (1989) work at the time, he suggested that corporations began to engage in a series of actions that changed the way the world worked. Calling it "flexible accumulation," he documented the ways that companies began to lay off workers and shift work to independent contracts. Newspaper articles documented how at the time workers would be laid off, and then hired back as a part-time contingent worker. Some individuals succeeded in this shifting landscape, marketing themselves as independent businesses and contracting their services. Others did not fare so well. At the same time, business and policy leaders were looking for ways to stimulate economic growth. And while there was little room to grow in the production of traditional goods, there was a push to deregulate financial systems and create a growing economy around finance and the buying and selling of financial services.

These pressures for financial deregulation, the elimination of the gold standard, and the restructuring of work and the workforce all produced the world that we know today. These forces also led to the patterns of deindustrialization in traditional industrial cities around the world. In the first phase of deindustrialization in the United States, industries moved from the north to the south. Eventually this led to globalization as industrial production did not cease, but moved to other countries where there were cheaper labor forces. These abandoned industrial landscapes will become important to the reimagination of urban spaces and craft brewing's place in the new city. These forces also led to the rise of liberal economic policy and ideas now rebranded as neoliberalism. Left leaning theorists saw the early days of neoliberalism as a response to the stagnation of the 1970s economy that would ultimately come into its own crisis (Foster & McChesney, 2009). As time went by, neoliberalism became more than just an economic policy, but rather a system for social control as it pressured all kinds of institutions to operate like businesses and to increase and measure their efficiency (Ong, 2006).

The crisis of the postwar welfare economy, or Harvey's Fordist/Keynesianism, has had a number of very contradictory effects. We can first talk about social class. The postwar economy, and postwar democracies were built on the idea of a large middle class. As economic growth got moving after WWII, many industries experienced rapid growth as they first rebuilt their economies, and then began to supply goods for the new postwar consumer economy. Labor unions grew and were successful in this period and many skilled laborers were needed and industry leaders were willing to share a small portion of the economic growth with workers, rather than slow down production and growth (Piketty, 2014). By the late 1960s, a larger percentage of the population in many industrialized nations enjoyed greater affluence and had access to benefits like education, healthcare, and vacation time. As the postwar economy stagnated, there was a loss of jobs, benefits, etc., as companies began to engage in the patterns of flexible accumulation. As Piketty (2014) suggests, as growth slows down, capitalists are less willing to share a portion of the limited economic growth with working people. At the same time, the information revolution (discussed below) created the need for more highly skilled workers, while it reduced the needs for skilled high-paid working-class workers. The effect of this is that the class system bifurcated. A number of organizations have been tracking these patterns but in effect the upper 2/5s of the middle class have increased their income and wealth, while the lower 3/5s have not. And in more detail the top fifth has grown a lot, the third fifth has remained somewhat flat and the lower two-fifths have declined significantly. The Pew Research Center, framing this as upper, middle, and lower income earners, has documented these trends and in 2015 the percentage of aggregate income for upper income earners has increased to 49%. While middle income earners, who used to command 62% of the aggregate income, are down to 43%.[1]

The trends have had an unusual impact on the economy. While most people have seen economic decline in the United States over the last 40 years, there is a sizable upper middle class and wealthy class that is looking for a more specialized and symbolically complex consumer lifestyle. No longer satisfied with the general affluence created by the postwar consumer economy, they seek more distinctive goods and services. And a portion of this desire has fueled interest in the farm to table food revolution, local wineries, coffee bars and specialized coffee products, and of course craft beer.

Another unusual effect of the crisis of welfare capitalism was the revitalization of ideas about entrepreneurship, creativity, and innovation. In the Information Revolution section, we will discuss Neff's (2012) work and her thinking about how workers in the tech industries shifted from a world where companies like IBM offered a work lifetime employment and assumed much of the economic risk to a world where employment was more precarious, and the economic risk was passed on to the worker. This shift is central to the economic reorganization that happened due to the crisis of welfare capitalism and led to the moment we now call neoliberalism. And as we saw above the further bifurcation of the middle class. Entrepreneurism and innovation have become key signifiers in the neoliberal moment. The postwar system was entirely about large corporations producing products for the masses. The quality of the consuming life was to be found in sameness, having the same car, house, boat, television, and beer as one's neighbor. It spawned the expression, "keeping up with the Joneses." But this new moment made room for specialization and creativity. Certainly, large corporations continued to dominate, but new products and services were encouraged by a public that was beginning to look for the new, exotic, and creative products to enhance one's consuming life. We can see that with early craft beer, the public was not quite ready for exotic beer flavors and styles, but by the 1990s these beers and the breweries that produced them began to take off. And, of course, Anheuser-InBev did what it could to make it difficult for these new small breweries to succeed.

While left leaning social theorists are very critical of the ideas, like innovation, creativity, and entrepreneurship, they are central to the craft beer movement. While much of the discourse around entrepreneurship is producing wealth and exacerbating the disparities between rich and poor, there is a counter movement where some individuals have sought to use ideas and techniques of innovation and entrepreneurship to bring about progressive social change. These individuals often work to transform notions of economic value and to innovate in order to make people's lives better. This work is often referred to as social entrepreneurship. And while the craft beer movement is not primarily about social entrepreneurship, it has been a movement that has sought to place different values, at least on the same footing, as economic value. These values include the quality of the product and the quality of the consuming experience. They also often include giving workers a greater share of the profit and a say in the process of production, as well as concern for the environment and other social issues. We will talk much more about these issues in Chapter 7.

The UK provides an interesting counterexample to look at alongside the development of the American craft beer scene. The UK and the United States experienced economic shifts toward neoliberalism around the same time, under Thatcher and Reagan, respectively. While these shifts had similar effects on capitalist production models, similarly, bifurcated the middle class, and similarly affected their consumption habits, the ideology of neoliberalism had very different impacts on the craft beer scenes in the two countries. The argument we will make for this difference is that beer culture has existed very differently in the two countries, with the United States experiencing a massive disruption and "reset" to its beer culture due to prohibition and its aftereffects. In contrast to this, the UK has experienced hundreds of years of cultural development for its beer in terms of consumption, culture, tradition, and taste. These important distinctions in cultural trajectory have greatly defined beer as a commodity and experience in the UK, often keeping producers beholden to traditionally appreciated styles to maintain profitability. Where, in the United States, it has provided space for creative experimentation and development in the production of craft beer as well as a curiosity for new and innovative beer styles among consumers.

## Globalization and the Political Economy of Consumer Capitalism

The crisis of the regulated capitalist economy drove businesses and policy leaders to seek a set of solutions to the problem. The first and overarching concern was to call for deregulation allowing businesses and financial organizations the freedom to move and let the market rationalize the economy.

Economic liberalization, or neoliberalism, had been around for most of the 20th century, but the ideas were not dominant during the era of Fordist-Keynesianism. The crisis of the 1970s brought these ideas back to the fore. And as mentioned above, one of the first moves was financial deregulation as in "allowed for the freer movement of capital and the potential of making money with money." This also led to some ironies that are still with us today as individuals and organizations are able to accumulate capital without any real contribution to the economy in the form of goods or services.

A second piece to the liberalization of the economy was the seeking of cheaper labor markets. Many of the industries such as automobiles were clustered in industrial cities with organized labor unions having a big impact on high labor costs and costs associated with worker health and safety. As businesses sought to find new labor markets, they began to move business from industrial urban areas to cities and towns in locations where there was no organized labor. In the United States, this meant that factories initially moved from northern cities into southern states in the United States. As the technological revolution continued to develop, it allowed industries to think more globally about the movement of businesses, and so many manufacturing companies would move their facilities to the cheapest labor markets. This is a phenomenon that continues to this day as manufacturing might move from one place to another multiple times over a short time frame, like a decade. This movement is the birth of globalization, which along with neoliberalism became the way people defined the world economy of the 1990s and until the crash of 2008.

A third piece to economic liberalization, and building on the new globalized arena of production, many companies began to seek new global markets for products and services. Many of these new consumers were workers who were working in the newly globalized industrial manufacturing facilities. These workers, while earning lower wages than the unionized workforces in the formerly industrialized north, had much more disposable income than they used to have. And so, these workers became a new group of consumers to market products to. Over time, as globalization advanced, many companies specifically moved factories to be closer to specific markets they were selling products to. And so, while General Motors moved assembly plants to East Asia for those markets, Honda moved assembly plants to the United States for the U.S. market. And by now automobile manufacturers, as an example, have assembly lines in multiple countries.

These three parts of economic liberalization and globalization – financial deregulation, seeking less expensive workforces, and seeking new markets – did not eliminate the problems central to capitalism and capital accumulation by the few. The contradictions of capitalism that were identified by Marx and Engels in the 19th century are still, in a modern and modified form, part of the process of capital accumulation. As we have seen in 2008, the global system went into crisis that was itself a result of the neoliberal solutions that were put into place in the 1970s and 1980s. This has left the current moment somewhat ill defined, but that gets beyond our purposes here. But this liberalization created the context for the entrepreneurial moment discussed above. And that entrepreneurial spirit was critical for the craft beer movement (as it was for the information revolution, coffee and cafe culture, wineries, farm to table food, as well as other industries).

This neoliberal moment did create a new opportunity for a "cycle of capital accumulation" as Arrighi (2005, p. 86) would frame it. And the capital produced by the financial liberalization of the early neoliberal era made it possible for the investment in urban spaces. It created the funding for public-private partnerships that built the urban consumer capitalist spaces that Florida (2005) discussed in his work on the creative class (Harvey, 2000). The transformation of urban spaces, discussed in detail below, will be central to creating the context for the craft beer movement, whether breweries were springing up in old industrial zones in large or small cities.

A further effect of globalization is that it helped spawn the anti-globalization movement, and movements like eco-consumption and slow foods. While consumer capitalism was evolving in profound ways, a part of the movement, as we have said before, was the bifurcation of the middle class and the tremendous concentration of wealth in a few hands. This inequality, coupled with a system that wasted energy and produced environmental disasters in order to manage the capital accumulation, spawned a number of movements that confronted the status quo. The most confrontational was the anti-globalization movement. It spawned a number of major protests around the world from the late 1980s to the early 2000s. There were also eco-consumer movements that attempted to model progressive change from within the consumer capitalist system.

Companies like The Body Shop, Ben and Jerry's, and others included environmental social activism as part of their business model. These companies, while sometimes being transformed into more traditional businesses over their histories, were looking for a model of ethical business practice. Craft beer can certainly be seen as influenced by these models and the reaction against globalization and traditional large-scale forms of wealth accumulation. As we have discussed early, probably one of the best examples of a brewery following this model is New Belgium. New Belgium was concerned for workers' rights, but located within a particular community, caring about the local environment as well as other local community concerns. And further, they were concerned about larger social issues too. New Belgium has and continues to seek a progressive path as an ethical business, even as it has grown into a large company now owned by a global corporation. Many other craft breweries, large and small, share many of these ethical and environmental concerns.

## The Information Revolution

At the very moment that corporations, government, and policy leaders were struggling with the stagflation of the 1970, the digital revolution was quietly beginning. The coinciding of the crisis in capitalism in the 1970s with the rise of the internet and microcomputing in the 1980s is one of those accidents of history that led to significant change. As computing and the internet began to expand their reach, this allowed businesses to further the changes that Harvey (1989) called "flexible accumulation." One of the early transformations that produced significant social disruption was General Motors' decision to move assembly plants from Flint, Michigan to Mexico. This was the subject of many articles in the scholarly and popular press, as well as the subject of Michael Moore's documentary film, *Roger and Me*. While a number of businesses were already moving out of the northeast and northern Midwest of the United States and relocating to southern states, moving out of the country was a bigger move and the beginning of globalization. This movement became possible because computers and the internet allowed upper management at GM to remain in Detroit and monitor the "global assembly line" from a distance. And this was not the only change, GM also involved people around the world in piece work assembling automobile parts in the home that would then get shipped to the assembly line as part of a "just-in-time" inventory system.

As the late 1980s moved into the 1990s, computing continued to have a significant impact on the U.S. economy and economies around the world. Digital technologies continued to develop and became more mobile, while server farms proliferated around the globe. This led to huge growth in computing businesses and the rise of what people called the dot-com boom. It also led to many high-paying jobs not only in computing, but in finance, management, and related areas, fueling the class divide discussed above. Interestingly, this was also the moment when a number of craft breweries began to take off. Not only had tastes changed as we mentioned in Chapter 3, but the new digital technologies helped craft breweries. We would argue that without the rise of the internet and digital culture, the craft beer movement would have likely been a much smaller and slower developing movement. An important way the digital revolution had an impact on craft beer is that it became central to the processes of production, distribution, and even consumption of craft beer. Digital tools made it very possible for small entrepreneurs to seek equipment and help in producing their product. They also are central to the advertising marketing effort as many breweries rely solely on social media tools. Finally, consumers who post their reviews to sites like Untapped become de facto part of the process of distribution as their reviews help sell a beer or a brewery to other consumers. We will talk about all these trends in more detail in Chapter 6.

The growth of dot-coms had several major impacts on the economy in general. The moves in the 1970s and 80s spawned by neoliberal economists, and conservative policy makers were designed to stimulate growth through patterns of deindustrialization and seeking cheaper labor markets. They also moved the focus of the economy from good production to financial speculation and consumerism. These moves, while producing growth, were small compared to the tremendous economic growth that happened during the dot-com era. Computing industries created real jobs and real growth. But further, speculation on computing the computer revolution led many to speculate that the business cycle had perhaps been overcome thanks to the ways that computers could make things more efficient and rationalize business practices (Neff, 2012). What many did not realize at the time was that the dot-com revolution was not overcoming the business cycle, but it was fueling a speculative bubble. There was a great deal of investment in every new technological venture and a faith that the growth that technology had brought about created a new era of constant growth. Of course, there was a lot of real growth, and many companies grew and succeeded during this period of time. But as Neff points out, there was an inevitable bust to the dot-com moment and considerable economic retraction. While the dot-com bubble and bust is not really the subject of our work here, it is important to note that craft beer too might be experiencing something similar, and we may be headed for a decline in the craft beer industry too. We already know that the COVID pandemic had a big impact on the volume of craft beer sold in 2020. But some in the industry see further downsizing coming too.

Neff (2012) discusses what she calls the rise of "venture labor" during this period of time. As discussed above, the postwar economy of "lifetime employment" for managerial employees came to an end in the 1980s. Neff discusses how 1994 IBM laying off or encouraging early retirement for a large percentage of employees was a watershed moment. These transformations in the global capitalist economy, due largely to the stagflation of the 1970s, would lead to what Neff calls venture labor, workers who take on more of the economic risk but gain a greater sense of freedom and entrepreneurialism. While Neff is talking about workers primarily in the information economy, the same could be said for the new craft beer workforce. While craft beer entrepreneurs came about a little before this moment in history, the late 1980s and 1990s were the moment when craft beer began to take off. And very clearly workers in the craft beer industry were venture laborers. This was not always true for every brewery, but it has been very true for much of the industry's workforce. Further, as craft beer became more popular, and idealized as a place to work, workers began to be willing to apprentice for free with the hope of landing a job as an assistant brewer and eventually maybe head brewer somewhere. While most of our informants got into the business when apprentices were being paid, and where they had the hopes of moving on to better jobs, there are a growing number of apprentices today who may be looking at less hopeful job prospects.

## Spatial Transformations

An important part of the rise of the information economy is the way in which space and time get rearranged. Several sociologists and social geographers have documented the ways in which space has been transformed as the information revolution led to the information society (Castells, 2001,

2010; Sassen 2001). Following the work of Lefebvre (1991), Harvey (2001, 2006) throughout his work has suggested that the different moments of capital accumulation in a capitalist system require a particular set of spatial arrangements. One can talk about the rise of the industrial economy as one involving the development of urban manufacturing centers and transportation systems moving materials to the industrial centers and manufactured goods from these centers. Most industrial cities from the late 19th to mid-20th century were structured in such a way.

As industrial manufacturing declined in these traditional urban centers and manufacturing was moved to new locations, these urban centers fell into disrepair. Many buildings and rail yards were abandoned. Workers moved out of the cities and into the suburbs as their jobs moved from manufacturing to service sector jobs. During this moment in time, from the late 1960s through the 1970s many futurists saw a world where cities were becoming less important. The emphasis was on the growth of the suburbs and even what people began to call the rurburbs for more rural suburbs. Cities were seen as a thing of the past and that left a lot of urban spaces that were ripe for renovation and renewal. The population of cities, like that of Philadelphia, are a good indicator of the urban process we are discussing. According to census data, Philadelphia grew to a high of over 2 million people living within the city limits in 1950. Subsequent census information shows a decline in population until the 2000 census where the population was a little over 1.5 million, a decline of over 500,000 residents. The largest percent decline was recorded in 1980, so the decade of the 1970s where the population declined over 13%. In the 2010 census and then again in the 2019 estimates, the city population has once again begun to grow but is still a little under 1.6 million. The decline in residents and the early movement of factories and offices out of the city left a large number of abandoned properties.

While deindustrialization and globalization initially created a context for the decline of cities, the further development of the information revolution created a new context for cities to flourish. For Castells (1989, 2010), cities are where the new information hubs are and the information workers who are critical to the global system. And while some cities are central to the management of this overall system, what we might call global cities (Sassen, 2001), smaller cities become regional hubs in the global system. What is different in this model is that smaller cities have some things in common with the small cities of old, but now they are more connected to the global system than they were before the digital era. The new global digital economy increasingly has become about flow, and these different flows must travel through nodal points, these points often being cities. Apadurai (1990) wrote an important article about this geographic rearrangement. For Appadurai, there were different "scapes" (think landscape) key, among them were mediascapes, technoscapes, ethnoscapes, financescapes, and ideoscapes, and these scapes were defined by their movement, or flow. The flow of media, technology, people, finance, and ideas traveled their own unique paths. The nodes (cities) where these "scapes" meet are each defined by what is flowing through that city and at what volume. So, cities right next to each other could be very different because of this unique process. Appadurai calls this disjuncture. There are many things we can take away from Appadurai's notion of disjuncture. One thing is that towns right next to each other might be very different because of the different flows of these scapes. Another point is that towns that are far apart from each other might be more similar due to similar concentrations of technology, finance, etc. An important point for us here, before the digital revolution, many "higher" taste consumables were only available in really large cities like Chicago and New York. But after the digital revolution, cafes, wineries, books, movies, etc., were much more widely available in smaller cities and towns. Elite culture could exist anywhere. In an earlier work, Shumar (2008) talked about what he called the commodification of cosmopolitanism. Part of that work discussed how cosmopolitan culture came to university towns in the form of high-end consumption. This is a theme we will take up in the last section of this chapter.

As cities large and small start being reimagined as nodes in the information society, the political economy of the city begins to shift as well. While traditional cities might have looked to bring in an industrial workforce and organize social services around that industrial workforce, increasingly cities seek to attract informational industries and the higher skilled workers that would be part of those information-based industries. Recently, Philadelphia was competing to be a second headquarters for Amazon. Philadelphia did not get the contract. However, as part of the discussions, it was pointed out that Philadelphia, (among several other cities) did not have a large concentration of "tech talent" (Adelman, 2021). While this is just one story, it is an indicator of the ways that cities are changing. A highly educated workforce, and especially a workforce that has a technical and financial education is especially valuable for urban development in the present moment.

Before the bursting of the dot-com bubble, Florida (2002) wrote a book about how cities now need to attract people who were part of what he called, the creative class. These are the highly educated, technologically savvy, innovative, and entrepreneurial workers who are willing to take on more risk and bring vitality to an urban information economy. Florida has received a lot of criticism for some of the limitations of his work. While we might want to moderate Florida's perspective, as big cities, especially, have a lot of different influences, the Amazon story mentioned above indicates that Florida is not completely wrong.

Important to our thesis, Florida (2005) argued that the creative class was not just technology workers, but also included artists, musicians, and other types of culturally creative people. The idea is that this class group is something of a taste group and their interests are more intellectual and highbrow. The creative class is highly educated, it has bourgeois tastes, and so cares about things like cafes, poetry readings, craft beer bars, and other high-end consumables. This group has also been called "bourgeois bohemians" by conservative commentator David Brooks. Brooks, as a conservative tends to see culture as the source of social problems and inequality rather than political economy, has also been criticized for his focus on this social group. One could argue that Brooks, and to an extent for Florida, have created this notion of the bourgeois bohemian rather than naming a group that really exists. But there is an element of truth in their analysis.

As cities seek to attract businesses like Amazon to locate new headquarters in their city, the presence of a more highly educated technical and financial workforce is a great draw. And of course, these are the more highly educated workers who have done well and are part of the upper end of the middle class, as the middle class has bifurcated over the last 30–40 years. In that context, urban space gets completely reimagined as they are structured to accommodate new forms of capital accumulation in the digital era. And so, old factories, which were once a blight on the landscape, now become imagined as the facades for beer halls, urban wineries, coffee roasters, high-end restaurants, etc. And blighted urban neighborhoods become the spaces where new high-end townhouses and condominiums are erected. Philadelphia, before the pandemic, experienced rapid gentrification in most of its poorer urban neighborhoods creating a dizzying transformation of urban space. Another example, in the UK, and at a slightly earlier moment, Birmingham England experienced the same kind of dizzying transformation in the 1980s and 1990s (Hubbard, 1996). With EU funds, the 19th century factories and the canal system became the backdrop for a set of urban transformations that turned the space into a combination of shopping districts, hotels, restaurants, music venues, and tourist walking tours. While the details are different from city to city, around the world these processes of urban redevelopment and the transformation of space were occurring.

Craft beer certainly has become part of this urban redevelopment. Craft beer, like a lot of craft products, was locally produced, artisanal, and concerned with the aesthetic quality of the beer-consuming experience. And so, brewpubs and taprooms associated with larger craft breweries were often in these new urban consumer landscapes. In the larger consumer economy, spaces moved from the large shopping centers that were cathedrals to consumption (Ritzer, 1999) to more fragmented and specialized consumer space. And urban spaces were perfect for these more specialized and higher end consumer spaces. One cannot see the craft beer movement as separate from these spatial transformations in consumer capitalism.

In the next section of this chapter, we will focus on the taste revolution that was also happening in consumer capitalism. But here, while talking about space, these urban consumer spaces certainly appealed to the high end of the income bifurcation that the Pew Center reports on. Craft beer was more expensive and specialized than the mass consumer market for beer. And while craft beer was always a smaller part of the beer market, from the late 1990s through 2019 it was the growing segment of the beer market, and an exciting part of the lifestyle of the urban cultural creatives' world.

## Transformations in Consumer Culture (Taste Revolution)

In this section of the chapter, we will focus on the shifts in consumer culture since the 1990s and the moment in the late 1990s and early 2000s when craft beer really begins to take off as a new product. While that is our focus, we will first discuss some of the longer trends in consumer culture and some of the theoretical assumptions that have guided research into consumer culture. One traditional view of consumer culture is that it is a result of the rise of capitalist production. In this view, we could see the beginning of mass production creating the context for a growing consumer culture. By the 19th century, factories were able to produce more consumer goods and luxury items such as cutlery, pottery, textiles, and consumables became necessary goods defining the basic needs of people in society. In this model, we could see capitalism, or the market system, as evolving through stages where the emphasis at first was on mass production, but later, especially after WWII, the emphasis in the capitalist economy was on mass consumption to meet mass production.

There are certainly ways in which the traditional model of seeing production coming before consumption is useful. One sees in the early 20th century the development of what we might call, following the general ideas in Foucault's work, "technologies of consumption." The late 19th and early 20th century saw the birth of modern advertising and mass media vehicles for that advertising like national magazines, and then later of course radio and television (Ohmann, 1987). However, a lot of contemporary research has focused on how consumption preceded production in the development of modern capitalism (Sassatelli 2007; Slater, 1997). Slater and Sassatelli, as well as others, point to the pioneering work of the French historian Ferdinand Braudel and his *longue durée* model of capitalist development. For Braudel (1979), capitalist development begins as early as the development of trade routes and markets in the late Middle Ages and early renaissance. Slater points out that Braudel tends not to talk about capitalism, but capital and capitalists. Trade produced capital that then capitalists (people who had capital) were beholden to. While we would argue, as we think most would, that the production of capital and capitalists over time developed cultures that we could call capitalism, Braudel's point is still an important one, that capital, produced through trade and markets, came before capitalism.

This idea of being beholden to the capital that one produces will actually work into our thinking about the beer economy. We would argue that one thing that happened to large breweries like Anheuser-Busch is that they became beholden to capital and the need to guarantee return on investment. Small craft brewers were able to prioritize product over capital, basically because they did not have much capital. But as craft breweries get bigger, they become more beholden to capital.

Central to the notion that consumption preceded production is the theoretical point that consumption is not a matter of satisfying needs, but rather a symbolic act (McCracken, 1988). Economic ideas about consumers being rational self-maximizers or making rational choices, assumes that need is a simple matter. The famous early 20th century anthropologist, Bronisław Malinowski, pointed out that all people need food, but what is considered food varies greatly among the cultures around the world. And so, consumption is always, even when satisfying basic human needs, a symbolic act. Mintz (1986), in his excellent historical study, *Sweetness and Power*, nicely showed how the symbolic nature of consumption shaped the development of the sugar markets in Europe and how slave-based sugar production helped to produce the capital to fuel the Industrial Revolution. In Europe, Mintz tells us, early on sugar was primarily used as a spice, a medicine, and a preservative. It was very expensive and so distinctive of wealth as a symbol. As the plantations in Barbados began to produce more sugar, the upper class used it to create cake monuments to their superiority. White sugar was a symbol of purity and racism, where the white races saw themselves as superior to other races. The symbolic value of sugar made it desirable to the middle classes and as economies of scale lowered the prices, middle class families sought to have a sugar bowl on their table as a symbol of their increasing affluence and importance. Eventually this worked down even to the working class where Mintz points out that the irony of the work break in a factory is seasoned with the products of the colonial empire, tea, and sugar.

The process that Mintz describes will become a common one in capitalism that every economist knows about. Often a scarce good, or new technology will start out as a prestige product. Over time, as economies of scale develop, the price is reduced, and more people can buy the product. Eventually with many products, they lose all prestige and become very low-cost basic products that are just part of the background of material life. Such was the case with digital watches for example. All of this discussion is illustrative of the symbolic nature of consumption and its primary place in economic activity. This is a concept we will return to when discussing value in Chapter 7.

Another aspect of the symbolic nature of consumption is its relationship to identity and social groups. The work of Bourdieu (1984) has had a major impact on research on consumer culture because of Bourdieu's theoretical concepts of habitus, social field, and distinction.

There are many reviews of Bourdieu's work and numerous social scientists implementing a Bourdieuian analysis. So, there is no need to explain the basics of Bourdieu's model here, but central to work on consumer culture is the way Bourdieu sees taste. His analysis of taste is that it is not only linked to social groups such as class, but tastes in music, art, etc., are in fact both the ways in which people make sense of the social world and articulate their identification with a particular social class fraction. Further, the tastes of other groups of people are often the ways individuals in different social groups conflict with each other, that is, "how could you possibly like that?" Craft beer, among a number of "consumables," certainly became distinctive of the developing educated upper middle class that Florida would call "cultural creatives," or Brooks calls "Bobos." This symbolic function of craft beer fueled the industry's growth as members of this social class were willing to pay twice as much for a beer than one would pay for a traditional domestic lager. Craft beer was a sign of cosmopolitan sophistication, while at the same time it maintained a fashionable hipster outsider signification as well. Craft beer could be both urbane and imagined as part of a working person's heritage. So, in a Bourdieuian sense, craft beer, like upmarket coffee, the farm to table food movement, and local wineries, became distinctive of a social class position and this taste marker helped fuel its growth. As we have seen above, this also fits into the transformation of the previous industrial landscape and into the digital revolution and its role in the realignment of social class groupings.

A limitation of the Bourdieuian perspective is its tendency to see the system of relationships as fairly static and the ongoing processes of social life as ones of reproduction. Boudieu's focus on fairly stable social positions may be a function of the period of time he did his main research. Lamont (1992) has also suggested that in North America, there are different tastes and values around which habitus is organized, and the class structure is less stable. Certainly, we have seen a proliferation of taste groups in the last 50 years that have led some sociologists to argue that traditional sociological notions of class are no longer relevant. We can certainly say that while the taste culture around craft beer could be seen as upper middle class, as that taste culture has evolved, it has both broadened and lost a kind of clear socioeconomic focus. And even thinking of it as a sort of hipster subculture movement in the 1990s and early 2000s that transcends class probably only has limited application.

Another important theoretical concern in research on consumer culture is the question of agency. Do individuals make their own consumer choices in the marketplace, or are they led to choose by larger and powerful forces such as mass media? With the rise of a mass consumer culture after WWII, members of the Frankfurt School were focused on ideological domination and how the public was being controlled by the new media technologies (Horkheimer & Adorno, 1947/2002). It is easy to see how the rise of a mass culture led by television led to the loss of public spaces and public interaction and to passive viewing. And so, people passively viewed in their own houses while drinking mass produced beer that was really not very distinctive brand to brand.

As the internet comes of age, it not only helps marketers target market segments and provide a more specialized consumer space, it also once again led to active individuals going to breweries and cafes, talking together, and being more active (Poster, 2001). This more agentic culture led to researchers questioning the passive nature of a public in a capitalist consumer culture. Researchers focused on a more active street culture and one that was not just responding to consumer symbols but also played an active role in the production of consumer culture (Miller, 2012; Willis, 1990). Thinking about consumption as a more active process, de Certeau (1984) suggests that consumption is a form of production because in the process of consuming people transform the meanings of that product or service. New meanings are produced through this process. de Certeau's ideas are not only prescient of the ways in which later researchers will think about concepts like "playbor" (Scholz, 2013) and "prosumption" (Ritzer & Jurgenson, 2010), but also very much describes the process of meaning and value production in the craft beer community. Consumers rate beers on platforms like Beer Advocate and Untapped. They tweet about their consumption practices and provide important information about beer festivals and brewery events. These activities are clearly producing symbolic value for craft breweries and can add up to a very important part of a craft beer's value. Miller (2012) takes a similar position on consumption to that of de Certeau. Coming from an anthropological framework, Miller sees exchange as a central part of all human relationships. We will see Graeber (2001, 2013) take up a similar line of thinking in Chapter 7. Social interaction and exchanges are fundamentally symbolic in nature and the social consumption/production dialectic begins with the meaning making exchange process. What Miller adds is that consumption and production are two sides of the same coin, the product and the consuming subject do not stand outside of this relationship.

## Craft Beer in Britain: A Comparison

The development of the English craft beer scene mirrors that of the United States, largely because the UK used the U.S. craft beer scene as a model to adopt and build on. The important difference between the two national beer scenes though was the state of commercial beer at the time. The United States had, and has, a distribution system where bars generally make the decisions about which beers and producers they would like to stock. They make these decisions based on relationships with breweries, and distribution networks, as well as what their customers demand. The UK model is not as laissez faire for those who own or manage a pub, or publicans as they are often referred to. UK pubs are often tied to, or owned by, certain brewery conglomerates and they are only allowed to stock and sell beverages from the breweries and distilleries that fall under that conglomerate's umbrella of ownership. Pubs owned by Fullers or Greene King or Youngs will only stock products produced by that company and its collections of brands. Most free houses (pubs that stock whatever they choose to) are smaller places with more limited buying power, who are also beholden to a complex system of interconnected breweries and distribution networks. This limits the options of what they can stock and generally also makes them pay a premium for it. An expense that gets passed on to the customer. This is the general UK pub model, but there are notable exceptions. Wetherspoons is a freehouse with nearly 1000 pubs under its control and an immense amount of buying power. This allows them to keep their prices much lower than their competitors.

To understand why this is the model that exists in the UK requires a bit of history. As far as the English are concerned, the UK's beer history is as old as recorded history. As such, what craft beer is often thought of as today is what beer was for centuries all over England. That is local, small-scale production, in rhythm with seasonal ingredients and tastes. Further, that community and communality that craft beer strives to produce was often also a by-product of this traditional style of beer production and distribution. The local pubs (tied houses and freehouses) served as community meeting centers, spaces and forums for public debate, occasional polling stations, and spaces to host many events for family and friends. Local Pubs were, and in some cases still are, the (largely male, heterosexual, middle class) community centers of their areas.

The beginning of the big breweries controlling production, distribution, and what was on draft at local pubs occurred during WWI in 1914 with the Defense of the Realm Act (DORA). This relatively simple act of parliament was used to ensure the war effort had all it needed, but also introduced the first licensing laws that were intended to be temporary measures. These licensing laws allowed the larger more well-positioned breweries to expand their holdings and diversify their markets (Gilbert & Smith, 1992). The effect was these breweries who had been able to obtain licensing rights and maximize their position through WWI came out of the war much stronger, while many of their smaller competitors went bankrupt.

WWII further decimated the independent English beer scene, as it did most of England. There was rationing and shortages of every commodity necessary to brewers, hops to glass and everything in between. This shortage extended beyond the war, but obviously the larger licensed breweries were able to weather this storm better and when the country and beer market recovered (by the 1960s) these bigger breweries bought up the resources and spaces left behind by those smaller breweries that went out of business. This meant that a few breweries were producing much of the country's beer. But possibly more importantly, some of these breweries had developed a massive country-wide network of tied-houses that they could use to exclusively sell their products. This even extended into the leisure market with breweries owning hotels, country clubs, and leisure resorts so they could monopolize those markets (Gilbert & Smith, 1992). This era of expansion by the big breweries and their buying of pubs to ensure distribution and profit represents the Corporatization and real estate-ization of the UK brewing industry.

In theory, this all came to an end in 1989 with the *Monopoly and Mergers Commission Report* (MMC).[2] In it "Parliament issued the Beer Orders which required the large brewers to cease brewing or free from purchasing tie half of the pubs they owned over the permitted number of 2,000 per estate by November of 1992. They were required to release the tie on all products other than beer and to permit licensees to purchase a draught cask conditioned beer from a source of their choosing." (Pratten, 2007, p. 613). While this was designed to break up the monopoly control the large breweries had on the market, the effect was not quite that. The tenancies were converted into long 20-year leases, the lessee who ran the pub now became responsible for all maintenance and repairs for the building, these pubs were still tied to specific breweries though, requiring them to buy breweries' products through "must stock" agreements in their leases. Further, there were penalties laid out in the lease if certain minimum beer sales or "barrelage" numbers were not met.

The neoliberalism of the 1980s saw the conglomeration of breweries and reorganization of their holdings, with as much of the costs of maintaining and running the pub as possible deflected onto whoever managed the pub. The motivating logic and unsavory business greed (which the craft beer community partially defined its values in opposition to) of the brewing industry of this era fit well with the Thatcher politics of the time. The big brewers used these government policies to their advantage and all but extorted their tied pub owners. This was all done in the spirit of neoliberal entrepreneurship and to create new business opportunities. Of course, this just resulted in higher profits and greater market shares for the big breweries, and greater costs and risks for the small pub owner.

The market consolidation from the 1950s through the 1980s made it clear to anyone who was paying attention that there were fewer and fewer producers out there. And while there may still have been an assortment of different beer brands on the shelves, consumer choice, in terms of producer, beer variety, and quality, was shrinking. This obvious-if-you're-looking observation is what led to the founding of the Campaign for Real Ale or the CAMRA movement. It was founded by beer drinkers who felt the increasing corporatization and shrinking choice in the beer market had made the beer worse and had a negative impact on consumer choice and freedom (Cabras & Bamforth, 2016). The CAMRA movement is decidedly the first step in the UK craft beer movement. It demanded traditional "real ale" beers (non-pasteurized, non-filtered cask conditioned ales pumped using hand pumps) be on draught at pubs. It also began to rebrand the CAMRA beer drinker as someone who was politically aware (at least within the confines of the beer world) and who respected tradition and traditional methods and values. This is still an ideology that is firmly in place in the UK craft beer scene. A dedication to craft and quality ingredients and a respect for brewing tradition builds the foundation of the craft brewing scene in the UK just as it does in the United States. But some modern craft brewers are beginning to look at the CAMRA philosophy as one that had a great deal of value for its time but is a bit of an anachronism now. Some modern brewers think the rigid parameters that the CAMRA movement demands of beer limits creativity and innovation, which stifles the craft brewing scene from moving nimbly in the market and from capitalizing on evolving and new beer interests (even if they are passing curiosities). Simply, some modern craft brewers think the CAMRA movement is too backward-looking in its approach to beer, too stuck on British brewing traditions to the point where CAMRA cries sacrilege when a beer does not fit neatly into their very traditional style guide.

While this feeling may have been brewing in the very small craft and homebrewing community in the UK before the early 1990s, until then there was very little, they could do about it. But by the early 90s, the MMC had done some work to open up space in the beer market for small craft producers to enter it. It was the opening of small local breweries that positioned themselves as serving their community that also allowed the UK beer market to "stabilize," meaning the number of breweries closing was matched or exceeded by the number opening. This moment in UK craft beer development is similar to the second wave of the evolution of the U.S. craft brewing scene. It saw breweries started by people who may not have a direct connection to the beer market (in terms of professional brewing or beer sales experience), but who are passionate about beer and very interested in producing a specific type of product. Many of these were experienced homebrewers, some were wealthy, or retired amateurs, and some were just passionate novice brewers looking for a place in the market. Some only produced real ales, some were more adventurous. Almost all of them though started out with beginner equipment or second-hand equipment they got used from closing breweries. While they may have been technologically limited, they did have one advantage previous small brewers did not, specifically the Beer Orders had forced the big breweries to free pubs from monopolistic ties. This meant many pubs that previously could only stock products from one producer could now stock the beers from the craft brewers of their choosing. This meant a great deal of opportunity and potential market share. It also meant the beginning of a cultivation of taste and affinity communities. But at the time craft brewers only represented a blip on the overall UK beer sales radar.

The seeds had been sown for the UKs craft beer movement to really take off. Today, it very closely resembles the craft beer market of the United States in terms of national market share, with UK craft beer accounting for about 5% of overall sales.[3] Similarly, the UK craft beer community has worked to increase the quality of beer available to the consumer, and they have worked to foster affinity communities around beer that act as knowledge-exchange groups and that encourage the integration of new craft beer drinkers. These breweries also work hard to maintain their individual values while brewing for the discerning beer drinker and also expanding the boundaries of stylistic traditions by offering creative and innovative interpretations of different beer styles. These innovations often present a kind of conundrum for breweries though. Stylistic innovations and creative interpretations of tradition are important characteristics that breweries need to exhibit if they want to maintain their position as a craft brewery. But these boundary pushing styles are often the least profitable, and not uncommonly the most expensive to make. Many breweries find themselves in a position where one of their more pedestrian beers is their best seller. Brewdog's Punk IPA, for example, is the best-selling craft beer in the UK, but some feel it is little more than a "kind of a gentle introduction into what craft [beer] can be" (field notes, 2019). The effect here is that breweries that find comfortable financial reward with a standard-fare offering still have to (or get to, depending on perspective) produce risky, boundary-pushing, and expensive beers to maintain their craft beer identity and membership within the craft beer community. Those who fail to do this risk remaining "craft" only in name alone, with any real connoisseur being aware that they are either a has-been or a sham. The American brewery Goose Island suffered this fate.

## Summary

An important theme of this book is the place of craft beer in the process of creating alternative forms of value. As mentioned, a couple times above, this will be discussed directly in Chapter 7, but this chapter sets the context for that discussion. One of our claims is that the craft beer movement, because of its place in time and space, was a kind of unintended social experiment where within a consumer capitalist framework, other values were dominant over the traditional business values of profit. The craft beer community values community, collaboration, a quality consumption experience, fair labor practices, environment, social equity, and more. And these values, in many breweries, are as important as making money.

A critical question, or set of questions are: what allowed this emphasis of other values to happen, what is the relationship to consumer capitalism, and is this just a utopian moment in the entrepreneurial process where the capitalist value of profit over all other values will reassert itself? This chapter has explored the political economic context of craft beer and has allowed us to frame these large questions.

As we have seen from the work above, the long evolution of consumerism under capitalism, the rise of digital technologies, globalization, and the reorganization of space from the late 20th century into the 21st century has allowed for what Arrighi (2005) might call a new run of capital accumulation. And so, craft beer, as a new cosmopolitan consumable within the new spaces of consumption, was made possible by these transformations within global consumer capitalism. At the same time, capitalism itself has been evolving, and an important pressure within capitalist culture is an evolution toward a more equitable and sustainable consumer culture. The craft beer movement has certainly been part of that push on capitalism and has involved the agency of many creative entrepreneurs with new visions of what a successful business might look like. The next several chapters will explore some of the details of this structure/agency dialectic in the craft beer movement.

## Notes

1 https://www.pewresearch.org/social-trends/2015/12/09/the-american-middle-class-is-losing-ground/)
2 The Monopolies and Mergers Commission (Performance of Functions) Order 1989, UK Statutory Instruments, 1989 No. 122, https://www.legislation.gov.uk/uksi/1989/122/made
3 https://toolbox-siba.co.uk/documents/Facts%20&%20Figures/SIBA%20British%20Craft%20Beer%20Report/The%20SIBA%20British%20Craft%20Beer%20Report.pdf

## References

Adelman, J. (2021). Philly came closer to being selected for Amazon's 'HQ2' than previously known, new book reveals, *The Philadelphia Inquirer*, published May 17, 2021. https://www.inquirer.com/news/amazon-hq2-philadelphia-brad-stone-unbound-andy-jassy-eagles-giants-20210515.html

Aglietta, M. (1979). *A theory of capitalist regulation: The US experience*. London: New Left Books.

Appadurai, A. (1990). Disjuncture and difference in the global cultural economy. *Theory, Culture & Society 7*, 295–310. https://doi.org/10.1177/026327690007002017

Arrighi, G. (2005). Hegemony unraveling - 2. *New Left Review* (33), 83–116.

Bourdieu, P. (1984). *Distinction: A social critique of the judgment of taste*. Cambridge, MA: Harvard University Press.

Braudel, F. (1979). *Afterthoughts on material civilization and capitalism*. (P. Ranum, Trans.). Baltimore, MD: Johns Hopkins University Press.

Cabras, I., & Bamforth, C. (2016). From reviving tradition to fostering innovation and changing marketing: The evolution of micro-brewing in UK and US 1980-2012. *Business History*, *58*(5), 625–646.

Castells, M. (2001). *The informational city: Information technology, economic restructuring, and the urban-regional process*. Oxford: Blackwell Publishers.

Castells, M. (2010). *The rise of the network society* (2nd ed.). Malden, MA: Wiley-Blackwell.

de Certeau, M. (1984). *The practice of everyday life*. Berkeley, CA: University of California Press.

Florida, R. L. (2002). *The rise of the creative class: And how it's transforming work, leisure, community and everyday life*. New York, NY: Basic Books.

Florida, R. L. (2005). *Cities and the creative class*. New York, NY: Routledge.

Foster, J. B., & McChesney, R. W. (2009). Monopoly-finance capital and the paradox of accumulation. New York, NY: Monthly Review Press.

Gilbert, D. C., & Smith, R. (1992). The UK brewing industry: Past, present and future, international. *Journal of Wine Marketing*, *4*(1), 19–27. https://doi.org/10.1108/eb008590

Graeber, D. (2001). *Toward an anthropological theory of value: The false coin of our own dreams*. New York, NY: Palgrave Macmillan.

Graeber, D. (2013). It is value that brings universes into being. *HAU: Journal of Ethnographic Theory*, *3*(2), 219–243.

Harvey, D. (1989). *The condition of postmodernity*. Oxford: Basil Blackwell.

Harvey, D. (2000). *Spaces of hope*. Berkeley, CA: University of California Press.

Harvey, D. (2001). *Spaces of capital: Toward a critical geography*. New York, NY: Routledge.

Harvey, D. (2006). *Spaces of global capitalism: Toward a theory of uneven geographical development*. London: Verso.

Horkheimer, M., & Adorno, T. W. (2002). *Dialectic of enlightenment: Philosophical fragments*. Stanford: Stanford University Press. (Original work published 1947).

Hubbard, P. (1996). Re-imaging the city: The transformation of Birmingham's urban landscape. *Geography*, *81*(1), 26–36.

Lamont, M. (1992). *Money, morals and manners: The culture of the French and the American upper-middle class*. Chicago, IL: University of Chicago Press.

Lefebvre, H. (1991). *The production of space*. Oxford: Basil Blackwell.

McCracken, G. (1988). *Culture and consumption: New approaches to the symbolic character of consumer goods and activities*. Bloomington, IN: Indiana University Press.

Miller, D. (2012). *Consumption and its consequences*. Cambridge: Polity Press.

Mintz, S. (1986). *Sweetness and power*. New York, NY: Penguin Books.

Neff, G. (2012). *Venture labor: Work and the burden of risk in innovative industries*. Cambridge, MA: MIT Press.

Ohmann, R. (1987). *Politics of letters*. Middletown, CT: Wesleyan University Press.

Ong, A. (2006). *Neoliberalism as exception: Mutations in citizenship and sovereignty*. Durham, NC: Duke University Press.

Piketty, T. (2014). *Capital in the twenty-first century*. (A. Goldhammer, Trans.). Cambridge, MA: Belknap Press of Harvard University.

Poster, M. (2001). *What's the matter with the internet?* Minneapolis, MN: University of Minnesota Press.

Pratten, J. D. (2007). The development of the modern UK public house: Part 3: The emergence of The modern public house 1989-2005. *International Journal of Contemporary Hospitality Management*, *19*(7), 612–618. https://doi.org/10.1108/09596110710818356

Ritzer, G. (1999). *Enchanting a disenchanted world: Revolutionizing the means of consumption*. Thousand Oaks, CA: Pine Forge Press.

Ritzer, G., & Jurgenson, N., 2010. Production, consumption, prosumption. *Journal of Consumer Culture*, 10(1), pp. 13–36. Available from http://joc.sagepub.com/cgi/reprint/10/1/13?ijkey=KKTk6xYE6Vq1c&keytype=ref&siteid=spjoc&utm_source=eNewsletter&utm_medium=email&utm_campaign=1J22

Sassatelli, R. (2007). *Consumer culture: History, theory, and politics*. London: Sage.

Sassen, S. (2001). *The global City: New York, London, Tokyo* (2nd ed.). Princeton, NJ: Princeton University Press.

Scholz, T. (2013). *Digital labor: The internet as playground and factory*. New York, NY: Routledge.

Shumar, W. (2008). Space, place, and the American university. In J. Canaan & W. Shumar (Eds.), *Structure and agency in the neoliberal university* (pp. 67–83). New York, NY: Routledge.
Slater, D. (1997). *Consumer culture & modernity*. Cambridge: Polity Press in association with Blackwell Publishing.
Willis, P. (1990). *Common culture: Symbolic work at play in the everyday culture of the young*. Boulder, CO: Westview Press.

# 5 Knowledge Production and Social Reproduction

## Introduction

In Chapter 2, we told a story about our travels to a conference where we shared some of our ideas about the new research project we were starting on craft beer, its dependence on new media, the informal knowledge production process, and the ways alternative forms of value were being created. And we remember that a colleague chastened us not to draw too solid a line between craft brewing and homebrewing. That recommendation, that we begin to brew beer ourselves, as we said in Chapter 2, moved this project from just being an interview project to one that was more ethnographic as we found our place in the wider community. Here in Chapter 5, we want to talk about the ways that homebrewing has been the training site for craft brewers and has also been the site of significant knowledge production for craft brewing. As such we think of homebrewing as the "invisible college" of craft brewing. We will get to that a little later in the chapter.

Craft brewing really began with homebrewing. The early craft brewers were the ones who were figuring out recipes, finding equipment, learning about yeast, and starting to make beer. In Chapter 3, we talked about how Charlie Papazian's homebrewing classes and the later publication of his book, *The Complete Joy of Homebrewing*, was central to the craft beer and homebrewing communities (Papazian, 1984). So, at the core, learning and practice were central to craft. Also, as we saw in Chapter 3, some of those early beers and breweries did not work out. But as we moved from the 1970s to the 1990s and early 2000s, many of those homebrewing entrepreneurs were finding success in transitioning to craft beer and creating craft breweries. Along the way they started also building a knowledge economy around brewing and running a brewery. In this chapter, we will highlight the many points of overlap between craft brewing and homebrewing, as the creative process of brewing begins to build the knowledge base of a new industry.

This movement from home brewer to craft brewer is a significant theme in the craft beer community. It is not the only way that people become craft brewers. Some apprentice with other craft brewers to learn the trade. Many people do both. One powerful story comes from Minnesota where Omar

DOI: 10.4324/9781003109686-5

Ansari began homebrewing in 1994 and was the founder of Surly Brewing. Apparently, he really loved making beer and he was really good at it. Surly Furious is a very popular IPA that has a reputation way beyond the St. Paul, Minnesota area where you can get it. It has a BeerAdvocate rating of 95 making it "world class" in their language. It has 5912 ratings as of August 2021. This is a very highly rated beer. After making a name for himself as a home brewer, Ansari apprenticed at New Holland Brewing in Michigan in the early 2000s. He started Surly Brewing with the help of Rock Bottom Brewing of Minneapolis after the apprenticeship. Surly rose to national fame when they proposed buying a new facility and raising 20 million dollars to create a brewery and pub connected to the brewery. In Minnesota, brewers were not allowed to sell their own beer in a pub setting, which threatened to nix the plan. Surly took on the issues and got the law changed in Minnesota. The new law became known as the "Surly bill" and there were a large group of fans supporting the new bill known as "Surly nation." The Surly story shows how quickly home brewers become craft brewer and rise to national prominence. There are other stories like this.

In Chapter 3, we talked about a brewpub in an older suburb of the Philadelphia region, which is a relatively new micro brewpub that is considered one of the outstanding local examples of the craft beer culture. It was founded by two colleagues, one who was a home brewer and went to the UK to study how to make cask conditioned ales, the other apprenticed at a larger brewpub in the area where he honed his skills making Belgian ales. These two brewers bring the apprenticeship tradition to their own establishment and while their beers are very inventive, they retain much of the tradition. Several of the English style ales are at cellar temperature, cask conditioned, and on hand pulls. While this is very normal in the UK, it is unheard of in the United States. The pub became one of the top beer places in the region. It has a good review from the city's top food reviewer and received some local awards. This is enough to bring not only beer enthusiasts to the pub but lots of others as well. On a weekend night in the past, you were likely to see a very odd mix of hipsters and older established folks all looking to sample beer and see what all the fuss is about.

The two brewers nicely illustrate different educational trajectories. The Belgian brewer, as stated above, apprenticed with one of the area's most well-known brewers. Interestingly, apprenticeship occurred at one of the more commercial craft beer brewpubs in the area. This is not an entirely uncommon occurrence though. These types of commercially successful (and sometimes corporately modeled) establishments often get highly skilled brewers to work for them. The establishment pays the brewer well and the brewer is comfortable with that as a long-term arrangement. But those less-well-paid brewer's assistants, who work for the paycheck and also for the experience and mentorship of the head brewer, take the lessons they have learned and sometimes use them to start their own brewery. This is, of course, a great risk. But it also offers these brewing entrepreneurs freedom, creative ownership, and the ability to profit directly from their labor. For some brewers, the corporate commercial brewing world can feel stifling. The mentor in fact left the more commercial brewpub citing artistic differences. One of the assistants went on to cofound the current establishment. He developed his skills as a brewer of Belgian beer through this apprenticeship relationship. The English brewer began with a homebrewing kit. Training as a glass blower and an artist, his interest in beer led him to the UK where he took a university-level training in cask conditioned ales. The very long history of brewing as both a cultural and commercial enterprise has resulted in many UK universities offering courses in brewing, either directly through courses in brewing and distilling or through courses skewed toward brewing in biochemical engineering or something similar. These two came together to establish their own brewpub and the result has been a well-deserved fame in the metropolitan region.

Most of the brewers we interviewed had similar stories. Most started out as home brewers, and then apprenticed at one or more craft breweries before becoming a brewer or head brewer. As more colleges and universities develop curricula for brewing, we expect that many more brewers will have university training in the future. But, of course, many of them will begin as home brewers before enrolling in a university program whether it be a degree program or a certificate program. When we look back in the history of the craft beer movement, most of the brewers started as home brewers. Some individuals who started breweries, like Jim Koch, were not brewers themselves but hired brewers to brew for the brewery. And Fritz Maytag ended up buying Anchor Brewing but was not a brewer himself. But as time moved on, many if not most craft brewers began their careers as home brewers. So, homebrewing has a very big part in the development of craft beer. And as we have said before, the coming together of the legalization of homebrewing, the development of the internet, and the transformations in the political economy discussed in Chapter 4, all had a hand in fueling the development of the craft beer movement.

In the next two sections, we will talk about some theoretical ideas that are important to the notion of informal knowledge production that can happen in community organizations. These ideas will help us think about knowledge production in the craft beer business. We will then move on to talk about homebrewing and its role as the "invisible college" of craft brewing.

## Invisible College

The idea of the invisible college goes back to Robert Boyle, William Petty, and a few others who founded the Royal Society in England in the mid-1600. Boyle and colleagues were in the process of pushing for dramatic cultural change in what defined valued knowledge and the ways in which knowledge was produced. Following the ideas of Bacon, the Royal society was focused on induction and empirical verification, practical real-world matters, and a scientific language that was spare and transparent. This very much conflicted with the Aristotelian focus of the traditional university curriculum (Purver, 1967). And so, this group of scholars were really fostering a new culture that was forced to develop outside the university.

In 1972, Diana Crane, a sociology professor at the University of Pennsylvania, published a book titled, *Invisible Colleges: Diffusion of Knowledge in Scientific Communities.* As a sociologist of knowledge, Crane (1972) was interested in the ways that informal networks of scholars produced work outside of an institutional context. Further she was interested in the ways that members of such informal networks saw themselves as part of something large, and perhaps even the ways that this informal structure formed its own unique culture and community.

Drawing on Crane's work, Paisley (1972), thinking about the idea of invisible colleges in educational research, suggests that the invisible college is a necessary concept when thinking about contemporary research. Paisley locates the invisible college within a larger structure that moves from a global level of culture, social, and political systems, down to very local networks within a researcher's institution and department. In this way, he is able to show how national policy, cultural ideas within a field of work, institution culture, etc., influence the process of producing knowledge. A critical, and more informal part of that framing is the invisible college. He sees it as similar to an individual's sociological reference group but organized more around a set of shared ideas (Paisley, 1972, p. 6) and we would add values. While the larger systems might constrain and shape the production of knowledge, the invisible college is the informal structure that fuels the creative production of new knowledge.

With the dawn of the internet era, this idea of the invisible college became more prominent in the thinking of different scholars. The internet provides the backbone for a dynamic group to share with each other in real time and all become part of the same virtual space (Shumar & Madison, 2013). The sharing of ideas allows for informal groups to have a more formal structure. There is evidence in many fields that the internet has fostered the rapid growth of new knowledge. In Chapter 6, we will look at the multiple ways that digital tools have fostered the growth and sharing of knowledge in the craft beer industry, as well as supporting other aspects of the business. The idea of the invisible college, an informal structure of individuals sharing ideas, is similar to two more contemporary notions, the idea of the community of practice (CoP) and the idea of affinity groups and affinity spaces. We will turn to these ideas now.

## Communities of Practice and Affinity Spaces

*Situated Learning: Legitimate Peripheral Participation* is a small book that when it came out had a big impact on social learning theories both within and outside of the field of education. In the book, authors Lave and Wenger (1991) tell us that apprenticeships are really different from the kinds of formal learning contexts that researchers see in schools where most education research takes place. But they suggest that there are things about the kinds of interactions that go on in apprenticeships that are very interesting as learning interactions and may have significant implications for theories of learning and knowledge production in other contexts. They were thinking of not only schools and universities, but also knowledge production that goes on in companies and other kinds of organizations. Lave and Wenger's little book was a very important book because it took the next step in the development of social learning theory. Vygotsky (1934/1978) and his followers had identified how individual learning was a social process and that individuals learned in a social context. But Vygotsky's focus was on how the social shaped the individual. Lave and Wenger were more focused on the social group and how the practices within that group were structured and how learning and knowledge production were a product of that group's activity.

Because of the kind of work they were doing, Lave and Wenger saw those groupings as communities – communities of practice (CoPs) – and there were different kinds of group membership, core community members who were the "old heads" and then newer members who learned the trade being practiced in the group. And these newer "legitimate peripheral participants" were very important for several reasons. First, they were the hope for the future of the group. They reproduced the group by taking up the trade and continuing the practice. But second and most importantly, they were the source of new innovations and new ideas. Without them the group's knowledge did not grow. Graduate students very much play this role in academic departments and academics are acutely aware of how the future production of knowledge and the future of the department and the field are dependent on the movement of these new legitimate peripheral participants from periphery to center.

The model of the CoP is rooted in ideas of practice theory. Traditional ideas about learning and knowledge production were that the processes were cognitive, even when groups were working on the same ideas, inventions, or innovations. But in the CoP, knowledge sharing, and the creation of new knowledge, happens through practice. It is not that some of the knowledge is not in people's heads, but rather it is made active by engaging in an activity in the world. Knowledge is shared and built on as people engage in the practice, talk about what they are doing, share with others, and experiment with the practices.

Central to Lave and Wenger's focus on practice are the ideas of French sociologist Pierre Bourdieu. Bourdieu's research focused on how social reproduction happened through a structure he called habitus. Bourdieu defines habitus as "durable, transposable dispositions" (Bourdieu, 1977, p. 72). For Bourdieu, habitus is a structure. Individuals are shaped by their community of origin and then that shaping is how they structure their social worlds as they go forth. This idea has been very important in research on education, but also in research on consumer culture too. It gives researchers a way to understand how taste is not random, and also important to the structuring of different aspects of social life. In the CoP, novices are inculcated into the practices of the group and so this has an impact on their habitus. But also, the novice's habitus from their community of origin (e.g., class and family) will affect how they receive the training in the CoP and further shape the practices and knowledge in that community. This intersection is the source of new knowledge. If we see craft breweries as CoPs, we can see how this intersection as novice brewers become legitimate peripheral participants can foster new recipes and styles of beer. Further, there are many collaborations between homebrewers and craft brewers in this process.

For years, after Lave and Wenger's book, researchers looked for CoPs in schools. Projects worked to develop CoPs. People tried to facilitate student CoPs, teachers and researchers worked to create teacher CoPs. Schlager and Fusco (2004) pointed out that one reason there was so much talk about the creation of and searching for CoPs in schools was because they were so scarce. A little later, Gee (2005, 2009) put together a critique of CoP suggesting that CoPs were very organized and structured communities and rather what exists in education, and other social worlds like gaming groups, is more like a shared space where people with similar orientations, interests, and ideas might come together. Gee called these "affinity spaces."

With the notion of spaces of affinity, Gee has at once captured something important for schooling but also something important about contemporary society. In schools, Gee points out that in the same class one student is trying to be very good at science and another student is trying to just get through school. And his question becomes where the CoP is, or are there multiple communities or is this not a worthwhile concept. Gee goes on to suggest the students who share a similar social space with others including teachers and experts in the field could in fact share a space of affinity and these spaces could be places where resources and practice are shared, and identities are developed.

While these insights are valuable for schooling, there are wider principles at play here too. Maffesoli (1996) has tried to capture the development of these new forms of organization with his notion of the neo-tribe. Maffesoli suggests that our globalized consumer society has broken down the traditional kinds of groupings and identities such as state and community and what we are left with are connections with each other that are becoming more like affinal and consanguineal ties that one might find in traditional tribal structures. There is a loss of a modern form of structure in this postmodern vision but there are positives as well. At the core of these new groupings is a tendency to produce new kinds of organization that are based more in a shared set of interests or goals and are less tied to traditional boundaries be they institutions, physical communities, or states.

Certainly, the rise of craft communities could be seen as part of either of these models. A key question for us is how to frame the craft beer movement in the United States. On the one hand, it has elements of the traditional apprenticeship community. On the other hand, the community is a neo-tribe and an affinity space. We would suggest that it is helpful to see craft brewing as a knowledge industry and that both the CoP and affinity spaces are models that are helpful to understand craft brewing as well as its relationship to homebrewing. Certainly, individual breweries are like CoPs. We have interviewed people at larger craft breweries where there is a team of brewers. In these breweries, they function exactly like communities of practice where the older (longer in the community) and more superior brewers pass on the knowledge of brewing and the practices within that brewery to the newer, "legitimate peripheral participants" in the brewery.

Many craft breweries have experimental brew systems that are often 1–5 barrels and not part of the regular production system. In two breweries where we interviewed brewers, the small systems are the place where different brewers could experiment with new recipes and new techniques. Some breweries foster their own internal competition ranking the experimental beers that are produced on the small systems. These beers are often sold only at the brewery's own bar and as sold as specialty items, often highly valued by customers who make the trip to the brewery to get beers they could not get in their corner store or bar. This internal process not only develops new knowledge in the CoP, but it is a way that different brewers can distinguish themselves.

Further, craft brewers in local areas are often friends and colleagues. They help each other with problems, they meet to talk about the business. They also are part of a network of relationships where when one moves on to a different job, a colleague often comes in and takes up the job in the old establishment. This network of relations is a broader CoP that a brewer might belong to. One of our informants told us that in the past, brewers and breweries needed to rely on each other for help with equipment, yeast supplies, and other things. This informant felt that while they could still reach out to a colleague if needed, it was less common today as many things they need are readily available from supplies. Further, they felt they were a little too busy these days to hang out with other brewers.

Beyond the brewery and the local network, there are larger affinity spaces that craft brewers are part of. Some of these spaces are formal meeting spaces for brewers such as national competitions or national meetings. There are regional organizations too. Sometimes, brewers will move across the country and bring the ideas from one part of the country to another. There is a large national and even international culture around craft brewing where brewers, in Gee's sense, share values, beliefs, a sense of taste and style, all of which adds up to something more like an affinity group. Affinity, as well as CoPs are important models for thinking about craft beer organization.

## Homebrewing

Below, we will turn to the ways homebrewing and homebrewers are part of the larger affinity space of craft beer. In June of 2016, Homebrew Con was in Baltimore, Maryland. As ethnographers, this was the first Homebrew Con any of us had attended. Since then, we have attended several Homebrew Cons. Homebrew Con is the annual conference of the American Homebrewing Association (AHA). The American Homebrewing Association sponsors a national beer competition and Homebrew Con is where the winners in different categories are announced, and where the overall winners of the national competition are announced. Beer competitions are very important to brewers. Beer competitions for craft brewers are valuable symbols of quality that might be important for their business. Beer competitions are important to homebrewers too. It is where they practice their skills and work to get better at brewing. Brewers not only compete but they train to become judges. That training provides them with skills that will help them evaluate their own beers as well as evaluating beers for the community. It is a place where the community's interest and the individual's interest meet. The AHA sponsors the Beer Judge Certification Program (BJCP). This is the formal training for individuals to not only become judges, but to set up local competitions. And there are many beer competitions in every community. It is the standard way by which brewers become better brewers. The scores and awards one gets from official beer competitions are analogous to grades one gets in school.

One evening, before the official conference had begun, a distributor of beer supplies sponsored a small party in a local bar for the owners of homebrew shops that he supplied. As we had developed a friendship with a homebrew shop owner, we were invited to go along. The event was very low key, all men as many beer events were, and really focused mostly on shop talk. During the evening, one shop owner, complaining about the general treatment of homebrewers in the craft beer industry, talked about how homebrewing had really been the educational system for craft brewing. He did not use the words "invisible college," but his argument was really about homebrewing being the invisible college of craft brewing and that Homebrew Con was the central conference for this invisible college. He focused on, as we have said before, how most craft brewers began and learned to brew by being home brewers. And homebrewing continued to be the pipeline for new talent and new ideas in craft brewing.

The following days, we attended Homebrew Con and began to see what the shop owner was talking about. Homebrew Con is the annual conference of the American Homebrewing Association. Like most annual conferences, it is in different cities each year. The conference is interesting as it is something of a cross between an academic conference and a trade show. There are several evening events, a keynote speaker, a homebrew club night where different clubs serve their beers, an award ceremony for the award competition, and dinner. During the day, there are different sessions. These sessions run from very applied to very scholarly. There is often beer to sample in sessions. One of the main draws of Homebrew Con is that it is where the winners of the American Homebrew competition are announced. As we said above, the National Homebrew Competition is the premiere beer competition for home brewers. It is analogous to the World Beer Cup or the Great American Beer Festival for craft brewers.

In 2016, we attended sessions on mash and water chemistry, several sessions on the microbiology of different strains of yeast, and a very sophisticated session on the tensions between hops and sours. There were sessions on the history of different beer styles, the evolution of wild strains of Brettanomyces, and more. There were also more applied sessions on cask conditioning, homebrew clubs, mead making, etc. Many of the speakers at Homebrew Con had PhDs in different or related fields. Usually brewing and the science of brewing was a hobby even if they were experts in the field. What surprised us as researchers was how much this gathering was an informal educational community where people were learning at a pretty high level. The sessions met a host of different needs among the attendants from people who wanted to really understand the chemistry behind mash chemistry, for example, to people who wanted to taste different kinds of beers and learn a little about how to make better beer in different styles.

Several of the top speakers at homebrew con, like Michael Tonsmeire, are highly respected in the industry. Tonsmeire is an economist by training, avid homebrewer, and author of *American Sour Beer* (Tonsmeire, 2014). He has one of the most respected homebrewing sites, The Mad Fermentationist. Tonsmeire has specialized for years in sour beers and wild fermentations. He does a great deal of creative experimentation. His book *American Sour Beer* is an important book to have for any brewer. Tonsmeire is not only willing to provide advice for homebrewers, but he consults for craft breweries and has collaborated with several craft breweries including helping Modern Times Beer Company develop their sour program. Tonsmeire is not only a great example of the knowledge and skills that is produced in the homebrew movement and shared at sites like Homebrew Con, but he is also a good example of how homebrewing and craft brewing overlap. While he has a career as an economist, he also has a career as a consultant and at least part time craft brewer.

Beyond major meetings like Homebrew Con, another important location of informal learning for homebrewers (and future craft brewers), as well as a place where homebrewing and craft brewing blend, are homebrew club meetings. Homebrew clubs are in many ways informal organizations. But at the same time, most are registered with the American Homebrewing Association, so they have a status as a local community organization fostering homebrewing. Many homebrew clubs are sponsored in some way by a local craft brewery or homebrew shop. Craft breweries often donate space for homebrew clubs to meet. They also might provide a free or discounted beer for dues paying members on nights when the club meets. Finally, the craft brewery might sponsor a talk about their work or a tour of the brewery for new members.

Homebrew clubs have an elected board. One of the main jobs of that board is to organize activities for the club. One of the activities is to sponsor monthly talks from individuals who can bring much of the same kinds of ideas and knowledge as one would get from the sessions at Homebrew Con. One local homebrew club in the Philadelphia area had talks from local scientists who were involved in the microbiology of yeasts, and the chemistry of making beer. These talks were at a pretty high level of intellectual activity. The club also helped organize members who want to train as BJCP judges and got them information about local training that was going on. There are also many other kinds of talks at homebrew clubs. Clubs will always share beer that members have been brewing and the more expert members who have been through judges training will often offer a review of a member's beer and suggestions for improvement. Clubs sponsor their own in-club competitions, several homebrew clubs in a local area will band together and create a competition. There are also larger regional competitions that homebrew clubs will encourage members to submit their beers to. Clubs often engage in friendly competition with each other to see which club gets the most awards at a particular competition.

In one homebrew club we observed, it was hosted by a local brewpub. The assistant brewer regularly attended the meetings of the club. The head brewer would occasionally come to give a talk at the club as well. One of the members of the club eventually became an apprentice at the brewery. Another homebrew club we observed the owner and head brewer of a small brewpub not only provided meeting space for the homebrew club, but would occasionally brew with homebrew club members, especially those who had award winning recipes. These beers would be specialty beers that were served at the pub's bar. Winning an opportunity to brew one's beer with craft brewers is one of the sought-after prizes when winning a beer competition for one's beer and the recipe for that beer. Very serious homebrewers will use these opportunities to make the transition into craft brewing and maybe get a position as a brewer's assistant in a local craft brewery. In the past, these positions were always paid positions. But as the number of individuals seeking to become craft brewers has increased, some of these positions have become unpaid internships. This heating up of the marketplace for positions has been making the apprenticeship road to becoming a craft brewer longer.

Several brewers find their way to craft brewing, not through apprenticeship but by increasing the volume and intensity of their own brewing activity. We opened the chapter with a story about Omar Ansari, the founder of Surly brewing. Ansari went from homebrewing to creating his own microbrewery on the property of his own parents.[1] We have seen similar brewing trajectories among some brewers in the Philadelphia area. And several of the big craft breweries that started in the late 1990s or early 2000s are built this way. Not through apprenticeship but through an evolution of a particular individual's (or several individuals) brewing practice. Beer brewing has a natural tendency to get larger. To a certain extent, if you can scale up your brewing operation you can do a number of different things. These days, you can buy better equipment. You can harvest yeast and maintain your own brewhouse yeast. You can set up more professional brewing operations. But as one moves from 5 gallons to 10 gallons, to 15 gallons to half-barrel system, whole barrel, and 5-barrel systems, you need to do something with all the beer. Many avid homebrewers donate beer to festivals and events, some brewers even give some beer away. But the process naturally leads to selling beer. And for the individual, they undergo a personal transformation that moves from homebrewer to a brewer identity. Individuals see brewing beer as their form of creativity and discover their own entrepreneurial potential. It's a major identity shift that can feel like personal growth. This process may involve a lot of invention and personal creativity. But it will also involve informal learning from a number of different potential locations. We will talk about some of those routes below.

Our study began as we realized that review sites like Beer Advocate, RateBeer, and Untapped are really informal education sites. With thousands of beer reviews, they represent resources for an education in taste. If the BJCP training formally trains one to be a beer judge, these websites can begin the process of informally training individual palates to the different flavors and styles of beer. At the same time, these sites are also the product of the labor that the consumer puts into building the community as they are both consumer and producer. These are ideas we will discuss more in later chapters. Beer Advocate is probably the broadest of the rating sites in that it has many different kinds of discussion lists, and not just ways to review beer. There are discussions on different aspects of brewing, beer trading, beers in different parts of the world, etc. Beer Advocate is simply one large site. But there are many sites for homebrewers. There are sites with recipes, diagnosing brewing problems, discussion about yeast, hops, malts, water, etc. If a brewer has any kind of brewing question or issue, the internet has a solution. There are also many YouTube videos that will take you from extract to full grain brewing, show you how to build a homemade mash tun, how to follow a recipe, etc. So many brewers rely on the resources of the internet to advance their learning in beer brewing and related topics. Both homebrewers and craft brewers find community, resources, equipment, and other things through the internet. We have argued that the craft beer industry would have not existed were it not for the internet. Chapter 6 is devoted to discussing the importance of the internet and digital media to craft beer.

Homebrew shops are another important learning resource for homebrewers as well as places to meet and collaborate with craft brewers. It is in the interest of homebrew shop owners to bring new brewers into the community. And so, they sponsor a number of outreach opportunities. Most participate in two AHA events, the Learn to Brew Day that is normally in November, and the National Homebrew Day that is in May. While the focus of these days might be novice brewers, especially the Learn to Brew Day, many more seasoned brewers who are associated with the shop will come out and also some of the local craft brewers who are friends and colleagues with brewers and the shop owner. Shops also sponsor brewing classes, help coordinate BJCP judges training, and put on local competitions. They often work closely with homebrew clubs which again are often connected to a local craft brewery.

Finally, we should say a few words about formal institutional training in brewing. Some of our informants have suggested that while homebrewing and apprenticeship will remain important in the craft beer industry, we will increasingly see more university-based formal educational programs and maybe other institutional programs as well. There are several reasons for this. First, as craft beer grows and there is more interest in the industry, there is a great need for trained individuals to work in that industry. But further, as breweries get bigger and maybe have more than one location, a consistent product becomes very important. Consumers want not only innovative beers, but they also want a particular beer to be identifiable, especially if it is a favorite. And so, consistency becomes more important as breweries grow beyond the innovative neighborhood pub. And consistency requires more rigorous brewing and adhering to scientific and technical methods that help produce a consistent product. And even further, as the risk of contamination and spoilage lead to bigger losses, again more scientific and technical methods are needed to guarantee the product. Formal educational programs can organize the scientific and technical curriculum that will produce different kinds of skilled workers, not just brewers, but also areas like quality control. They will certainly continue to be the small breweries that do not need these skills, or occasionally hire outside consultants for these needs. But it is clear that in this way, craft beer is becoming more like the larger brewing industries.

## Themes

We have tried to paint a picture of the many ways knowledge production is organized in the craft brewing industry. And in this process, we have shown the close connection between homebrewing and craft brewing. While increasingly there are more formal beer training programs in universities and in the brewing industry, to this day, most of the training and knowledge production in craft brewing has been informal, and we see informal knowledge production as continuing to be central for craft brewing. Across these different loci of knowledge production, we see some larger themes that also influence the craft brewing world. We will conclude this chapter with some of those themes. And these themes will come up in other chapters as well.

An important theme in the book is the ways craft beer, as an industry and a culture, is entrepreneurial and inventive. The recent pandemic has seen many small craft breweries shift from selling beer out of the brewery or brew pubs bar to canning beer, distributing to stores, and even creating delivery services to get beer to people. Craft breweries, especially small ones, are very nimble and quick to respond to the marketplace. Many began to can beer and deliver it by car or pickup truck to customers around the region who ordered through the website. Homebrewing is a place where a lot of this innovative and entrepreneurial spirit begins. Homebrewing begins for most people as a small, 5-gallon batch operation. Most of the equipment is simple and even homemade. Homebrewers love to make mash tuns, plate stirrers for yeast, brewing systems with pumps and tubes to connect the various tanks. Because of this it is possible to be very experimental with one's brewing. The risk of loss is very low. This allows the homebrewer to focus almost exclusively on creativity both in terms of the beers one makes and also in terms of the processes. If one wants to add more unusual additives to a beer just to see what happens, that is very possible. If a brewer wants to experiment with Brettanomyces either by purchasing wild yeast from a yeast provider or cultivating wild yeasts in one's own kitchen, there is not much to hold a brewer back from these experiments. Brewers can experiment with barrel aging because they are only waiting on their own beer. That means that the homebrewers who do become craft brewers have a lot of innovative experience and are very focused on creativity and innovation.

Beer is a knowledge industry. What started the success for Jim Koch and Boston Brewing was that he had a good recipe for a beer. That recipe was important intellectual property. For many craft breweries, the recipe for their main beer is critical. But of course, so many other aspects of the industry require knowledge. Many early breweries had trouble with maintaining tap lines and controlling contamination. We can think of the knowledge that exists as both conceptual but also the practices and skills that are used within a particular brewery, or by a particular brewer. And that is why we began the chapter with the ideas of communities of practice and affinity groups. This knowledge exists within overlapping circles of relationships among people within a brewery, between breweries, and with the large community including homebrewers.

The creativity in this knowledge industry is what has made craft beer so dynamic. In a few short years, we have gone from lagers to Belgian style beers, to the domination of the West Coast IPAs, to New England IPAs, then back to lagers, and many other styles in between. And as each of these styles come about, they must be debated within a tradition that defines a particular beer style in a particular way. There is a very interesting dialectic that agitates in the craft beer community between tradition and innovation. Tradition is a route to proving one's expertise as a brewer. Awards are coveted and reinforce one's identity as an excellent brewer. Further, brewers have a real appreciation for tradition and a beer that is an excellent example of a style. If one can successfully reproduce an in-style award winning Belgian dubbel, for instance, that is a sign of one's skill as a craftsperson. But what people are looking for in the community is innovation and interesting new tastes, the creation of new styles. And in the United States, this dialectical tension is very dynamic and moves very quickly. New England IPAs are a good example of this tension. The New England style is so different and interesting that it does not fit within the style guide for IPAs from the BJCP. At the same time, these beers were a very big hit. Some have argued that the solution to the problem is that NEIPAs are a new style of pale ale, just not an IPA. But there continues to be tension in the community, while it is clear the beers are very popular. These tensions of legitimate knowledge and its products will be explored in more detail in the chapter on values.

## Summary

Whether we are talking about very large-scale high-tech industries like the airlines, dot.com booms, or the craft moment, practice and learning are much more tied up with the world of work in the 21st century than they have been in the modern era. That means that so many workspaces are becoming learning spaces and they are tied up with knowledge production. Apprenticeship is often the model for these learning organizations or some combination of apprenticeship with other knowledge building activities. And in these work situations, individuals are encouraged to be more creative, dynamic, and entrepreneurial. This is true whether we are talking about the new Chrysler Corporation, Airbus, or craft beer.

Returning to Lave and Wenger's (1991) idea of CoP as a model for learning, we'd like to suggest that there is a new way we can think about how apprenticeship is a model for learning. Craft beer is an industry where we have overlapping modes of interaction. Each brewery is clearly a CoP and apprentices learn the practice through the brewing of beer and interaction with the more senior members in the community. Perhaps this is why craft breweries prefer a more informal structure, something that is a benefit to collaborative work, but as we have seen recently has its own dialectical tensions.[2] At the same time, apprentices go out and work with, or establish new breweries. And there are overlapping networks of homebrewers and craft brewers who contribute to the dynamic innovation in the field. So, craft brewing is also a space of affinity that has a looser structure and is built more on a set of shared feelings and values and not a community organizational structure. Craft beer needs both of these models of knowledge production to be successful.

Craft is not only a new way to live, but it is transforming production and consumption. This transformation is something that some have tried to capture in the name of prosumer (Ritzer & Jurgenson, 2010). And prosumers are part of a new world that is putting practice and learning at the center of many productive organizations. Production spaces are becoming spaces where people apprentice and learn. The interests and motivations of the workers are paramount to the success of the organization and so they are creative spaces of consumption too. This is true whether we are talking about a gourmet food truck, a craft brewery, or a larger industry. And as Neff (2012) points out, there are clearly problems with this new model, especially for workers in large-scale organizations and industries where there are great concentrations of capital. But there are many potential benefits of these changes that could not only take greater advantage of human potential, but also allow more surplus value to remain with the producers of goods and services and for that capital to remain in local communities. Potential is obviously not what will be. But nevertheless, it is important.

The importance of the craft beer movement and the informal learning that is core to this movement is far greater than just this one sector of the economy. It has implications for bigger transformations in consumer capitalism. In the next chapters, we will explore these transformations, the ways that digital media has made certain ways of working and being possible, and how new forms of value are created. Theoretically, the craft beer movement might have implications for knowledge production and learning, as well as changing toward a more human-centered economy.

## Note

1 https://tcbmag.com/honors/omar-ansari/
2 Part of Chapter 8 will discuss the recent problems of sexual harassment and sexism in the craft beer industry. In part, these problems have become a major problem because many breweries do not have a human resources department and way for employees to share file complaints and discuss harassing treatment.

## References


Bourdieu, P. (1977). *Outline of a theory of practice*. Cambridge: Cambridge University Press.

Crane, D. (1972). *Invisible colleges: Diffusion of knowledge in scientific communities*. Chicago, IL: University of Chicago Press.

Gee, J. P. (2005). Semiotic spaces and affinity spaces. In D. Barton & K. Tusting (Eds.), *Beyond communities of practice: Language, power, and social context* (pp. 214–232). Cambridge: Cambridge University Press.

Gee, J. P. (2009). Affinity spaces: From the age of mythology to today's schools Retrieved from http://www.jamespaulgee.com/sites/default/files/pub/AffinitySpaces.pdf

Lave, J., & Wenger, E. (1991). *Situated learning: Legitimate peripheral participation*. Cambridge; New York, NY: Cambridge University Press.

Maffesoli, M. (1996). *The time of the tribes: The decline of individualism in mass society*. London; Thousand Oaks, CA: Sage.

Neff, G. (2012). *Venture labor: Work and the burden of risk in innovative industries*. Cambridge, MA: MIT Press.

Paisley, W. (1972). The role of invisible colleges in scientific information transfer. *Educational Researcher*, *1*(4), 5–8+19.

Papazian, C. (1984). *The complete joy of homebrewing*. New York, NY: Avon Books.

Purver, M. (1967). *The royal society: Concept and creation*. London: Routledge & K. Paul.

Ritzer, G., & Jurgenson, N. (2010). Production, consumption, prosumption. *Journal of Consumer Culture*, *10*(1), 13–36.

Schlager, M. S., & Fusco, J. (2004). Teacher professional development, technology, and communities of practice: Are we putting the cart before the horse? In S. A. Barab, R. Kling, & J. H. Gray (Eds.), *Designing for virtual communities in the service of learning* (pp. 120–153). New York, NY: Cambridge University Press.

Shumar, W., & Madison, N. (2013). Ethnography in a virtual world. *Ethnography and Education*, *8*(2), 255–272.

Tonsmeire, M. (2014). *American sour beer.* Boulder, CO: Brewers Publications.

Vygotsky, L. (1978). *Mind in society.* Cambridge: MA: Harvard University. (Original work published in 1934).

# 6 Digital Media and the Possibility of Craft

## Opening Story

In June of 2012, as we were about to start our formal research on the craft beer project, we decided to systematically attend Philly Beer Week. We had gone to events that were part of Philly Beer Week (PBW) the couple of years prior. But we were then attending as fans and just looking for a couple of events that would be fun to go to. But now that we were planning to seriously study the craft beer community in Philadelphia, we decided that it was important to go to as many events as possible. As Philly Beer Week is a week-long celebration, it would not be possible to attend every event. But as there were three of us, we were able to divide up and attend a lot of events. The biggest day is opening day, which starts in the afternoon and continues into the evening. There was an opening event that required the purchase of advanced tickets. Then there were many events at different bars and public spaces around the city. A lot of people attend the opening events, especially in the evening so it felt very much like a citywide party.

Philly Beer Week began in 2008. Different media outlets state that it is the oldest and largest beer week in the country.[1] It has been the model for many other cities to create their own version of a beer week celebration. One story goes that celebrated author and beer critic, Michael Jackson, used to visit Philadelphia every March to meet up with brewers, restaurateurs, and bar owners. When he died, a core group of individuals decided to create Philly Beer Week as a celebration in his honor. After the first two years, the celebration was moved to June.[2] While the founders of Philly Beer Week were hoping to attract a few hundred participants, it quickly grew to an enormous citywide celebration with many venues, events, and individuals participating. It is probably the event that put Philadelphia on the map as a major "craft beer city." While the event is distributed throughout the city and suburbs over the week (usually a ten-day event), the *Hammer of Glory* is a physical symbol that ties the celebration together. Over the opening day, the Hammer is driven from venue to venue on a motorcycle. Its progress is tracked over Twitter and other social media.

DOI: 10.4324/9781003109686-6

On the opening day in 2012, we were tied up at the university with obligations until about 4 p.m. We then began to try and figure out how to participate in the event. At first, navigating the available events, as well as which ones would be best to attend was very unclear to us. There was a newspaper called City Paper that had a table of all the events and their locations and times. With City Paper in hand, we began to map out a plan as to where and how to go. We started to follow the hashtags #PBW and #pbw2012 on TweetDeck to see the things that people were posting. This first night of Philly Beer Week was the most popularly attended and included many events that gave this distributed week the feel of a community. Firestone Walker, one of our favorite West Coast breweries, was going to be at a bar downtown. Firestone Walker had built a reputation over a few years as an innovative brewery and one of the leading producers of the West Coast Style IPA. We found out about the event both from a schedule posted on the PBW website as well as from the tweeting activity around this event. Many people were excited to meet the heads of Firestone Walker and so the quest had the feel of an effort to see a celebrity. As we headed to the event, we started to see tweets that it was not possible to get within three blocks of this bar. We decided it made no sense to try to get to this celebrity status event. We also realized that many other people were way ahead of us in this quest and had made sure they had gotten to the bar early. It began to rain as we decided to abandon this event. We noticed that two key individuals in the #PBW feed had not only met up at the bar where Firestone Walker was going to be but also they got there early and got one-on-one time with the brewers. We were envious of their luck. We went to two other bars, neither of which turned out to have much activity.

As it started to rain harder, we decided to take a cab to a third bar: Devil's Den. Not because there was a specific event at Devil's Den, but just because it's a cool place, and an occasional host of PBW events. Devil's Den is considered one of the premier craft bars in Philadelphia, where the local "brewerati" of the craft movement sometimes imbibe. When we arrived, Devil's Den was packed but we pushed in through the crowd and toward the back for the bar. Amazingly, in the back we found a spot at the bar and began to look at the very nice beer list. One of us ordered a 4 Hands Red Ale. There was also a firkin of a sought-after sour beer, and we also got glasses of that beer. We were told their firkin was the only available small quantity of this beer to make it east of the Mississippi. While 2012 was four years into a dramatic increase in sales of craft beer, it was still a different time than now. People were excited about craft, opportunities to talk to brewers and owners was considered a rare opportunity. And people would line up to get a pint of a beer, such as Russian River Brewing's Pliny the Younger, which was only released in small batches once a year. Craft brewers have continued, with success, efforts to keep this kind of hype going with specialty beers and limited releases.

As we stood in Devil's Den discussing our beers, we struck up a conversation with a guy standing nearby. It was a very nice conversation and we felt part of the crowd as people pressed in all around us trying to get closer to the bar. He was very interested in what we thought about the 4 Hands Red Ale. As the conversation progressed, he revealed that he was the president of 4 Hands Brewing Co. Ironically, we saw over Twitter that the President of 4 Hands was at an earlier event where the two individuals who got an interview with the Firestone Walker people said they missed connecting with him. Something about losing out to these two strangers but accidentally scooping them on the meeting up with the president from 4 Hands made us feel like we were part of something, something bigger that had some kind of weird organization to it, even though all these events were largely disconnected. No other part of Philly Beer Week felt this much like one was part of a larger ritual of what Turner (1974) would call *communitas*. But the general feeling of community does permeate the whole weeklong event. Much of the driving force of PBW is encounters, sometimes serendipitous, with other people passionate about beer, while pursuing some, occasionally elusive, beer experience. Another way to talk about this interaction is to suggest that bonds of affinity are created through such a digitally mediated experience. Philly Beer Week is an affinity space where like-minded people feel they are part of something, even though the connection is only through this one set of shared tastes and interests. Further, the bonds of affinity exist within a distributed space that is both physical and virtual.

## Digital Media and Space

Boellstorff (2008) in his case study of Second Life suggests that there is always a "gap" between the virtual and the actual. Bucking a tendency in internet research at the time, Boellstorff did not like the binary virtual/real as for him the virtual is just as real as the actual. Even if this gap becomes very small, it is always still there and important to theorize (Boellstorff, 2008). On the one hand, the virtual is always part of the actual and that the actual is in fact a product of imagination (Anderson, 1991). And Boellstorff (2008) indeed acknowledges this. But on the other hand, there is another dimension to what Boellstorff is trying to suggest. In our digital world, increasingly we all work and live in hybrid social spaces where we have one foot in the virtual and another foot in the physical or actual. As we all construct hybrid social spaces, members of different communities can meet, work, and play together. But those hybrid spaces, while they might create one imagined landscape, do not "blur" the online and the offline. In fact, like Boellstorff suggests, they depend on the gap to create an imagined whole. Philly Beer Week was filled with gaps. Some intended, some not. Some seen as possibility, others seen as missed opportunity. But the social space depended on this gap and some of its creativity, serendipity, and lost opportunities were products of that gap. The excitement of Philly Beer Week, the sense of connection with others, the sense of creative opportunity, and belonging are all created by the gap and the ways that individuals navigate the gap.

The entire PBW space was one of affinity stitched together with various media (Gee, 2005). While all the media were important to this construction, we were particularly impressed with how Twitter both aggregates and individualizes – it depends on aggregate behavior, but also on individuals tweeting and searching the particularity of affinity group hashtags (Murthy, 2013). These affinity spaces are constructed both online and offline, and members engage each other in both spaces. Certain members – for reasons of luck, skill, or serendipity – navigate in some spaces more successfully than others; however, what is important is that to really be a member of the affinity group one must be an active participant in both online and offline spaces. Boellstorff's gap is experienced as the space of possibility and connection. But this gap is not experienced directly, rather it is experienced in the juxtaposition of the virtual, imagined, and actual. With many people running around the city to get to different events, and the Hammer of Glory traveling from venue to venue being tracked through Twitter by different participants, the whole evening appeared as a dream space, as the interaction between the virtual and actual warped our sense of space and time.

While opening night of PBW is particularly profound, the other days had a similar, although less heady feel to them. Further, many craft breweries participate in afternoon or evening-long beer festivals, tap takeovers, and other kinds of events that are designed to create excitement and raise awareness of craft beer, attempting to expand the community and the market for craft beer. All these events, to some extent, created the same kind of excitement and imagination that the opening night of Philly Beer Week creates.

Social scientists coming from a Marxist and critical perspective focus on the ways in which economic production requires a particular arrangement of social space. In the era of digital technologies and the internet, we not only see that production and consumption have particular spatial arrangements, but we further see that these new technologies allow for a warping of space and time that can have implications for production and consumption as well as meanings that are produced and identities that people take up. Herman (2013) suggests media consumers become "co-producers" of meaning and value and that spatial and temporal separations (such as work and home) increasingly become collapsed. In our experience of Philly Beer Week, we experienced these new warped spatial and temporal realities. The meanings that were produced during the events of Beer Week were themselves very much the product of the ways that Twitter and other internet sites created a social space. This was a space of play for the participants in the festival, but of course these were productive workspaces too (Ritzer & Jurgenson, 2010). And the interactions that were a weave of virtual and physical interactions were themselves part of the "co-production of meaning" that had value.

These ideas are very much in line with Lefebvre's (1991) ideas on the social production of space, as well as Harvey's (2006) rethinking of Lefebvre's model of space. And as Lefebvre would suggest, there is novelty in the way that citizens occupy that space, so while there are clear patterns for production and consumption, there is an element of the unexpected. The founders hoped for a few hundred participants, but they had no idea that they would produce an event that had thousands of participants and dozens of brewers and would be a model for advocating for craft beer in other cities. And finally, we are reminded that at the basis of this spatial transformation is the erosion of the productive spaces of the postwar system of industrial production and the transformation of decaying urban architecture and space into postmodern consumer spaces for the technological upper middle as discussed in Chapter 4.

About the same time, we were immersing ourselves in the experience of Philly Beer Week, there was an article in a magazine called Philly Beer Scene titled "The Twitter Effect" (Sterner, 2012). The article talked about how Twitter was becoming increasingly important for craft brewers. On a surface level, tweets are advertisements for beers, breweries, and craft beer events. But the article goes on to point out that as one tweets while drinking a beer, or hanging out at a brewery, or participating in a beer event, it deepens the meaning of the experience and creates a sense of connection among fans...literally it makes community (Sterner, 2012, p. 46). This work is, in itself, value production, but we will get to that later.

Philly Beer Scene was a glossy physical magazine that existed for several years. It then went online only, and the last post on their Facebook page was January 2018. The magazine's history mirrors the rapidly changing and growing craft beer market, and digital media's part in those rapid changes. In 2012, there was still a place for physical magazines. The magazine was free, and one could find it in just about every craft beer bar in the metro Philadelphia area. The article we are referring to here pointed out that many beer drinkers over 50 did not use Twitter and wanted to come into the bar to see what was on tap. There was a portion of the market that benefited from having an actual magazine to read about what was going on in the community. And the craft beer market benefited from physically reaching out to them. By 2018, there was no longer a sustainable niche for such a magazine. As more and more people went digital, and as social media became central to everyone's life, the magazine first went online but then disappeared altogether. Its function as an advocacy instrument for the craft beer market had been fulfilled.

While Twitter was important to craft beer, and continues to be important, other social media platforms have been equally important. In 2014 and 2015, Facebook was probably the most important platform for craft beer breweries. Most of our interviewees during that period pointed to Facebook as the main avenue for advertising their beers. One brewer told us that they could post a new special bottle release on their Facebook page and then the release could be sold out by the next day or two. Consumers paid close attention to the Facebook pages of their favorite breweries and were especially aware when something new was available. To this day, Facebook continues to be important for craft breweries, but many breweries get just as much traffic on their own websites. Over time, many more breweries also began using

Instagram. At first, brewers were a little unsure of how to use Instagram, even one brewer told us he liked to take pictures with Instagram but was not sure how to make use of it. Over time, as Instagram evolved, more breweries were using it to advertise their activities. As social media began to shake out generationally with many Facebook users being older, Twitter users being in their 30s and Instagram users being younger, breweries began to adapt a strategy of marketing to different generations of beer drinkers with these different sites. Of course, there is a lot of generational overlap in all media, but there are also these generational patterns. And the important thing here with social media is that it is not just posts that the brewery puts up, there is also a lot of user-generated content. And so, breweries will like posts that are about their beers and their breweries. The content is easy to produce, and community members contribute to the production. Again, we will talk more about this below.

There are also specifically platforms for users to post, rate, and review beers they have been drinking. Sites like BeerAdvocate, RateBeer, and Untappd are designed for users to post what they are drinking in the moment and then invites them to rate and/or do a full review of the beer much like a professional sommelier might review a particular vintage of wine. The marketization model for these sites is entirely about the value that users generate in their posts and their reviews of particular beers. This is another example of Herman's (2013) point that in the era of social media the production of meaning is tied up with processes of capital accumulation. These sites are not directly related to craft breweries, but they help in advertising the beers and breweries. They also deepen the sense of connection among craft beer drinkers, making them feel part of a community as they generate value through their activity.

These insights about the effects of digital media and the internet on craft beer producers and consumers led us to speculate that digital media was essential for craft beer as an industry and as a social movement. An interview with one of our informants brought this out. We were talking to the brewer and owner of a local brewpub in the Philadelphia area about the role of the internet. Our informant talked about a friend of theirs who was a craftsman. This friend's craft was the production of throwing knives. It turns out that throwing knives are a very specialized market. The brewer told us that before the internet, this craft would most likely be just a hobby, as there is not enough of a market in Philadelphia for throwing knives to sustain a business. But in the era of the internet and social media, this craftsperson has a thriving business. They have a reputation for making a very good product and people purchase the product through the internet from all over the world. Thus, the internet makes this entrepreneurial model possible. Craft beer is not nearly as specialized or esoteric as throwing knives, but the point here is that social media allowed a producer of a specialized product to advertise their product free of charge so that a particularly interested audience could find this product, discuss and determine its quality, and purchase it. This is very similar to how craft beer producers use social media, as a space that is equally for advertising their products and one that facilitates the social space to foster affinity groups around the beers they produce.

While in the digital worlds, production, distribution, and consumption are interwoven, for the rest of this chapter, for heuristic purposes, we will discuss each aspect of the craft beer economy and the ways that digital media have influenced the practices that people engage in. One wants to remain very aware that the notions of prosumption (Ritzer & Jurgenson, 2010) and digital labor (Scholz, 2013) really require that we see production, distribution, and consumption as interlinked and part of the same set of practices in the digital world. In the real world, it is probably not possible to separate the moments of production from consumption, but for analytical purposes, it is useful to talk about each separately. That said, moments of consumption, when one is drinking a beer and posting a review of it at the same time, are moments of production and consumption and this is part of what Ritzer and Jurgenson are talking about.

## Production/Distribution/Consumption

We argue that craft beer only took off as an industry thanks to the internet and digital media. Digital technologies have been central to craft beer's success. So, it is ironic that craft brewing is a very traditional manual labor process. It requires a lot of physical labor, lifting large, heavy sacks of grain and hops into brew kettles. There is a lot of sweating over the brewing process itself. And probably cleaning equipment is the most arduous of manual tasks that go into brewing. Many brewers define the brewing process as 90% cleaning, 10% paperwork, and the rest of brewing itself. This somewhat exaggerated statement is to underscore the irony that many brewers got into the trade for the creative side of coming up with an interesting recipe and brewing that recipe to get, hopefully, great results. But, in fact, the brewing, the part that the brewer and the public is interested in, is a small part of the process. Many times, when we were in a small craft brewery, we saw brewers in large rubber boots with cleaning equipment.

Beer brewing involves several different kinds of tanks. There is the mash tun, where hot water is added to the malted grains to extract the sugars and create a wort – the sugary liquid that will be boiled to make beer. There is the brew kettle where the wort is boiled, and hops are added. Boiled and cooled wort is added to fermentation tanks where yeast is added, and the beer begins to brew. And then there are bright tanks where beer can mature, clarify, and be carbonated. All this equipment needs to be cleaned regularly. And to avoid off flavors, the equipment is cleaned very carefully so that there is no residue, and then the equipment is sterilized so there are no yeasts or bacteria that are still lingering in the equipment and are not wanted.

In the early days of craft brewing, there was no manual for how this was done, and little opportunity for formal training as we have said. Brewers made accidental discoveries, like the key to the Belgian flavor in Belgian beers was the strain of yeast. In this early context, brewers were very dependent on each other for a number of things. And as the internet became more available, brewers could rely on the internet to help with supporting the community of beer producers. Several brewers told us they would travel to other breweries to learn what people were doing and share information. Increasingly, if a brewer had a crisis, such as a yeast pitch that did not work, they could reach out to fellow brewers over the internet to see if anyone had yeast they could share.

As we discussed in Chapter 4, most craft brewers began as homebrewers. This is still largely true, if changing. And homebrewing has a very substantial internet presence. Many brewers basically learn how to brew and how to troubleshoot problems over the internet. They learn different techniques, recipes, and styles that way too. Homebrewers are a good model of the producer/consumer regularly engaging in the process of prosumption (Ritzer & Jurgenson, 2010). They have taken up what at the beginning is a hobby and a consumer activity, and then become successful producers of beer. For many homebrewers, their desire to produce better and more interesting beer leads them to consume more equipment and to seek a wider audience for their beers. This is perhaps a different version of what Duffy (2017) calls "aspirational labor." All homebrewers aspire to making excellent beers, want an audience that reviews their beers, and some eventually want to make a living, or a portion of a living doing this work. Homebrewers contribute recipes and knowledge through the internet to other consumers of this information, as they consume the information themselves. This labor both enhances their status in the community as well as helps build their own expertise. The process, for some brewers, leads to the desire, or opportunity to become an entrepreneur and move the practice from homebrewing to craft brewing. Because of this kind of apprenticeship experience, many craft brewers inhabit a prosumer subject position that continues to inform how they see what they are doing.

In the early days, getting equipment was a challenge. Many brewers welded their own early systems. A market in buying and selling used equipment slowly emerged and again this marketplace occurred over the internet. As we said in Chapter 4, brewers share questions, challenges, and opportunities in discussion lists. This world of discussions did overlap between the homebrew and craft brewing communities. And equipment was an important part of that discussion. Many craft breweries as they grew would put older systems up for sale. There was also the necessary knowledge to operate different brewing systems and so many of those connections were made over the internet too. Some avid homebrewers who were really interested in brewing to scale would also look for half barrel or full barrel systems. While these are small for a craft brewery, they were often systems that people started out on in the early days or experimented with new recipes on. Small systems are still used for experimentation by craft breweries. An interesting trend that began to develop in the 2000s was the nanobrewery. While there is no hard and fast definition of a nanobrewery, they often have a boil kettle of three barrels or less. And it means they produce very small batches. Nanobreweries are certainly one way, especially in more recent times when there is already a number of craft breweries, that avid homebrewers make the transition from homebrewer to craft brewer. While Philadelphia has not seen a lot of nanobreweries, in some parts of the country, like Seattle, they are very popular. The nanobrewery also helps to further blur the line between craft brewer and homebrewer. Some small brewpubs are started by homebrewers, and their friends, maybe members of a local homebrew club, continue to help at the brewery or get an opportunity to brew their recipe at the brewpub. These things are all advertised through social media like Instagram and Twitter.

These experiences of the challenges of brewing coupled with the use of the internet to share information, equipment, and resources led a lot of craft brewers to be part of a local community. Here more than an affinity space, brewers would meet up, hang out together, and depend on each other. It fostered a sense that they were different from the usual business and "collaboration not competition" that became a popular catchphrase in the 2000s, the height of which was probably from 2010 to 2015. There were articles in the beer magazines and even more popular press about different breweries that were getting together to collaborate on a beer. Breweries still engage in these collaborative beers. These collaborations even became international as craft breweries in different countries collaborated. Mikkeller brewing, co-founded by Mikkel Bjergsø, is famous for not only being a driving force behind the development of the craft beer scene in Denmark, but also for collaborating with a few U.S. craft breweries. Bjergsø's brother founded Evil Twin brewing, furthering the sense of a connection between the craft scenes in the United States and in Denmark. Bergsø, in an early collaborative interaction with Alesmith brewing, bought their old facility in San Diego and opened the first Mikkeller brewing site in the United States (Rowe, 2016).

While these kinds of collaborations were critical to the craft beer movement as craft beer began to grow dramatically and support from colleagues was needed, one informant suggested these kinds of interactions are less common now. He suggested there is less need, and there is less time to hang out together. One example of how there is less need now would be to look at brewing equipment. In the early days, homebrewers and craft brewers were making their own equipment from found objects. Even as late as 2014, we put together our own mash tun using an igloo cooler and parts one would find from a plumbing supply rather than buying a mash tun. But now there are many manufacturers offering very good equipment from basic to high end. And there are not just brewing systems for homebrewers but there are 5–30 barrel systems available for the craft brewer with lots of options. Venture capital in craft brewing has become common, and so setting up a small craft brewery has become a much simpler process. In craft beer, there is still an ethos of collaboration, but also as the market tightens, the reality of competition with not just big beer, but with other craft breweries is becoming a reality.

Distribution, on one level, is also a very basic material process of distributing a manufactured product to a market. We saw that in the early days of craft beer distribution was one of the major problems for breweries as most distributors were beholden to Anheuser-Busch InBev (Ab InBev) and were unwilling to risk their main client by taking on smaller craft beer clients. We saw in the history chapter, breweries like New Belgium put beer in their car and delivered beer themselves. Many breweries did this. Ironically in the pandemic, one of the survival strategies was to go back to this kind of direct delivery. Hindy (2014) talked about how his brewery, Brooklyn Brewing, started their own distributing company to deliver their beer and the beers of other small craft breweries. Getting physical distribution of beer has been a challenge for breweries, and while there was a moment historically where craft beer was able to break InBev's hold on distribution, many small breweries still face this challenge.

On the other hand, as social media became more central to the digital lives of everyday people, the internet became the focus for marketing and advertising in the craft beer world. In 2010, Wired Magazine published an article "The Web is Dead. Long Live the Internet" (Anderson & Wolff, 2010). In this article, the authors discuss the movement from desktop and laptop computing, with their emphasis on accessing through the web, to the rise of portable devices, smartphones, and tablets, and accessing the internet through apps. This shift is also related to what has been called Web 2.0 and the rise of social media platforms like Facebook, Twitter, and Instagram. Originally, Web 2.0 was declared to be more participatory than Web 1.0. And it is certainly the case that the shift is about the massification of the internet. But one could argue that Web 2.0 becomes more participatory through particular platforms that frame interaction in ways that make wealth production more possible on the internet. And it does this in a few ways. The participation in media like Facebook, as we now know, allows for targeting marketing, the production of data that can be sold to companies and the use of interactions as means of advertising, marketing, and the creation of brand awareness.

Most of the breweries we talked to, including those that distribute across state lines, admitted that they have notably small marketing budgets. Social media platforms have become integral to the craft beer industry. All the breweries and brewpubs in our study use Instagram, Twitter, Facebook, and company websites to publicize what's on tap, announce new beers, and announce their special events to the public. They organize their brand awareness campaigns, such as raising awareness for breast cancer or other social good campaigns through a combination of social media. The marketing reps of breweries also do a number of events like tap takeovers, festivals, and beer weeks. All of this is community work as they not only reach out to the public through social media, but a dialogue is begun around a beer or an event. Many brewers will respond to a posting about one of their beers in Untappd. And consumers will push announcements about events or send out tweets or pictures from the event.

The work of interacting on social media can be an aspect of the consumption of beer, or an event. Some consumers of craft beer engage in beer trades that are organized either offline or online. Often Twitter has been an important tool for organizing beer trading. These trades are about the ability to pick up desired beers and share them with others, while hopefully getting beer that one could not easily get on their own. Different forms of consumption can be, at the same time, a form of production. It produces advertising and brand awareness. But also, it produces communicative signifiers, verbal or visual, that are themselves valued by members of the community, these are things like brewery or beer event paraphernalia, brewery or beer insignias, cherished slogans, phrases, and jokes understood by the in-group. They all have value for and to the group, and they are goods in and of themselves. This leads us from thinking about distribution to thinking about consumption and the ways these things are all related. In the craft beer world, there is much that the term prosumption explains. Ritzer and Jurgenson (2010) suggest that prosumer capitalism is a new phase of capitalist development. In the earliest age of capitalism, the focus was on the development of productive capacity, and after WWII the focus was on the development of a consumer society and consumer capitalism. While they suggest there was prosumption in those earlier phases, prosumption has become the dominant practice in the current era. For Ritzer (2014), prosumption is not originally or primarily about digital labor. Rather it is about using self-checkout machines in the grocery stores or bussing your own table in a fast-food restaurant. It is about passing some of the productive work on to the consumer who is in the process of consumption. Ritzer certainly does recognize that the digital world brings about new levels of prosumption. And he further argues that it is really capitalism that keeps these forms of prosumption from their progressive potential (Ritzer, 2014).

It's interesting to see that in craft beer, there is a lot of emphasis on traditional forms of production, it is a very manual labor-intensive practice. But as we have shown above, the semiotic production, the production of signs and meanings, don't just advertise the products they are linked to, they are values in themselves. And so, craft beer is very much part of the process of prosumption. But further, craft beer has come closer to realizing the more progressive potential of prosumption. One could argue that craft beer has not, so far, been a capitalist industry. The tensions between craft breweries and "big beer" are themselves a marker of the fact that most craft breweries are smaller, more local commodity producers. And, as we have suggested already and will expand on in the next chapter, craft brewers and craft breweries embrace the values of community, environment, the quality, and joy of craft production. Craft production is a value in and of itself. Perhaps this is why craft breweries have been so successful at embracing the power of digital tools. Prosumption helps their business, that is for sure, but prosumption also supports a wider range of values that the craftsperson seeks to uphold.

Nevertheless, craft beer is certainly moving toward capitalist production. And one could argue that some of the biggest companies, for example, New Belgium, Boston Beer/Dogfish Head, and others, are in fact capitalist industries. Most of those industries have sought some way to maintain their focus on craft production, and not just become another industry focused on capital accumulation. And so New Belgium became worker owned and then sought to maintain the existing structure with their contract with Lion Little World Beverages, which is owned by Kirin Brewing. And Victory Brewing and Southern Tier Brewing created a merger that would allow them to maintain their local focus as local craft breweries.

Finally, an important part of thinking about digital media and consumption in the craft brewing economy, and a part that is linked to the discussion about prosumption, is the idea of status consumption. As craft beer began to take off as an industry in the late 1990s and early 2000s, high-status beers have been an important part of the excitement and value in the community. In our Philly Beer Week story at the beginning of the chapter, shortly after we settled in at Devil's Den in South Philadelphia, we learned, as said above, that they had a firkin of a sour beer that many beer enthusiasts were excited to try. And so, we ordered glasses of the beer to taste its sour, fruity, bretty flavors. As we were drinking the beer, people told us this was the only firkin of this beer east of the Mississippi. Who knows if that was true. But what was important was that it had high value as a high-quality, exotic, scarce commodity.

We also mentioned in Chapter 3 that Russian River Brewing developed several very famous West Coast IPAs. The most exclusive of which is Pliny the Younger. Pliny the Younger is produced once a year. There is a very limited release and pubs that get a keg of Pliny the Younger are sought out. It is a Triple IPA with high specific gravity, meaning a lot of malt sugars went into making the beer and has an ABV of 10.25%. A rare, and strong, beer. Other big beers like Heady Topper and Dogfish Head 90 Minute IPA also excite the community. These beers become status symbols for the brewery and for the consumer. The same is also true for new styles of beer that attract the consumer looking for the latest and newest thing. Posting in social media that one is participating in the excitement of consuming a rare beer or reviewing a new style of beer early in the trend contributes significantly to the status of the brewery and the consumer at the same time. It is also free brand awareness marketing as we discussed above.

A theme we will take up in the next chapter is the tension between the meaning that status consumption produces, and the negative impact it could have on ideas like authenticity, legitimacy, and truly being a craftsperson who is seeking quality and craft, and not just aping those concepts as gimmicks to advance one's place in the market. As with all social media, there is the potential to support alternative meanings and values, and there is a potential to play to the lowest human interest and only create something we might call hype.

## Summary

The resurgence of craft is a movement that goes way beyond beer. Craft production includes food, wine, coffee, clothing, jewelry, software, and much more. These craft movements tend to be small. In the beer market, craft production is currently about 12.3% of the volume of beer produced. And while craft beer contracted more than big beer over the course of the pandemic, what has been alarming to organizations like AB InBev is that craft beer has been the only growing segment of the beer market.

As we have discussed in the chapter, new media has been at the core of modern craft beer from the beginning. Mediation is central to the production, distribution, and consumption of beer. As stated above, many craft beer brewers began as homebrewers. Websites abound with discussions and information about beer production. In our interviews, the majority of brewers told us that they learned a lot of things from online resources. There are ABV (alcohol by volume) calculators, sites that explain how to create a yeast starter, how to do whole grain brewing, etc. There are recipes posted online, discussions about how to deal with water quality, where to find brewing equipment, etc. Notably, one of the brewers in our study developed his brewery from his website activity.

Moving from production to consumption, beer festivals, tap takeovers, and tastings are an important social space where brewers and consumers get together and share their products with each other. For the past several years, these are increasingly organized and advertised online. Additionally, apps are becoming central to the craft brew movement. Apps such as Untappd construct digital social spaces where brewers and consumers share with each other what they are drinking and what they like about what they are drinking. And interactive websites such as The BeerAdvocate and RateBeer have enormous numbers of reviews of different beers and breweries, as well as other resources on their sites.

Finally, marketing is particularly important to the craft brewing movement. Most of the breweries we talked to, including those that distribute across state lines, admit that they have notably small marketing budgets. Social media platforms have become integral to the craft beer industry. All the breweries and brewpubs in our study use Instagram, Twitter, Facebook, and company websites to publicize their special events to the public. While in the early 2000s, older craft beer consumers were not as connected to social media, now all segments of the beer market are accessible through the internet and social media. Breweries organize their brand awareness campaigns, such as raising awareness for breast cancer or other social good campaigns through a combination of Twitter and Facebook. The marketing reps of breweries also do a few events organized through Instagram, Twitter, and Facebook.

In theoretical terms, we have discussed how digital media in the craft beer world has reorganized social space. Lefebvre (1991) talked about how social space is organized for production. Various stages of capitalist production required the reorganization of social space to make production possible. What looks to us like a normal or given order is really a particular arrangement for the run of capital accumulation. And these orders of space are very much transformed through the use of newer technologies (Harvey, 2006). But further, people creatively use space in ways that are not completely predictable. And so out of particular arrangements of social space emerge new practices. These are things we have discussed in previous chapters, and we see that digital media has helped to allow industrial spaces to be transformed into spaces of craft prosumption. These communities of producers and consumers of craft beer share a distributed space created through new information technologies where the production of craft beer and its audience both become possible. Further, the gap between the actual and the virtual enhances the meaning and excitement about craft beer. The gap also opens a space where consumers can be producers as they produce brand and marketing work for breweries as well as meanings about quality and experience that are valuable to others who have affinity with the community. Without these technologies, the space for prosumption would not be possible.

Craft beer is not only made possible through new media, it is also an example of digital labor (Scholz, 2013). The brewers and consumers participate together in a world where play, leisure, and labor become inextricably entwined with each other. And while it is an industry on the upswing, it is also an example of venture labor (Neff, 2012). Producers and brewers assume the risk of their ventures as they move away from the older large-scale corporate brewers. What remains an interesting question is where will this all go?

Finally, the excitement opened up by this craft economy that produced new stars in the form of creative brewers, new tastes, and a role for fans to be producers too, created a space for status consumption. And status was itself a new value produced by the craft beer movement. The new statuses produced both fueled the excitement in the craft beer movement, but also alarmed some practitioners that the industry was becoming too fixated with hype. This tension will remain an underlying tension in craft beer.

## Notes

1 https://breweriesinpa.com/philly-beer-week-makes-its-return-this-coming-june/ https://en.wikipedia.org/wiki/Philly_Beer_Week

2 https://billypenn.com/2016/05/29/the-story-behind-why-philly-beer-week-was-moved-to-june/

## References


Anderson, B. R. O. G. (1991). *Imagined communities: Reflections on the origin and spread of nationalism* (Rev. extended ed.). New York, NY: Verso.

Anderson, C., & Wolff, M. (2010). The Web is dead. Long live the Internet, *Wired*, August 17. Retrieved from https://www.wired.com/2010/08/ff-webrip/

Boellstorff, T. (2008). *Coming of age in second life: An anthropologist explores the virtually human*. Princeton, NJ: Princeton University Press.

Duffy, B. E. (2017). *(Not) getting paid to do what you love: Gender, social media, and aspirational work*. London; New Haven, CT: Yale University Press.

Gee, J. P. (2005). Semiotic spaces and affinity spaces. In D. Barton & K. Tusting (Eds.), *Beyond communities of practice: Language, power, and social context* (pp. 214–232). Cambridge: Cambridge University Press.

Harvey, D. (2006). Space as a keyword. In *Spaces of global capitalism: Toward a theory of uneven geographical development* (pp. 119–148). New York, NY: Verso.

Herman, A. (2013). Production, consumption and labor in the social media mode of communication. In J. Hunsinger & T. Senft (Eds.), *The social media handbook*. New York, NY: Routledge, 30–44.

Hindy, S. (2014). *The craft beer revolution: How a band of microbrewers is transforming the World's favorite drink*. New York, NY: Palgrave Macmillan.

Lefebvre, H. (1991). *The production of space*. Oxford: Basil Blackwell.

Murthy, D. (2013). *Twitter: Social communication in the twitter age*. Cambridge: Polity Press.

Neff, G. (2012). *Venture labor: Work and the burden of risk in innovative industries*. Cambridge, MA: MIT Press.

Ritzer, G. (2014). Prosumption: Evolution, revolution, or eternal return of the same. *Journal of Consumer Culture, 14*(1), 3–24.

Ritzer, G., & Jurgenson, N. (2010). Production, consumption, prosumption. *Journal of Consumer Culture, 10*(1), 13–36.

Rowe, P. (2016). Now open: Mikkeller San Diego. San Diego Union-Tribune (April 16, 2016). Retrieved 20 April, 2017, from https://www.sandiegouniontribune.com/entertainment/beer/sdut-mikkeller-san-diego-opens-2016apr16-story.html

Scholz, T. (2013). *Digital labor: The internet as playground and factory*. New York, NY: Routledge.

Sterner, B. (2012). The Twitter effect: How social media shapes beer. PHILLYBEERSCENE.COM, pp. 43–46.

Turner, V. (1974). *Dramas, fields, and metaphors: Symbolic action in human society*. Ithaca, NY: Cornell University Press.

# 7 Values and Value Production

## Opening Story

Early in our research one member of our team went to do an early interview with a brewer from a local brewpub in Philadelphia. His wife went along for the ride. It was a very cold winter night near Christmas, temperatures were around 11°F. It was so cold that the bar was not very crowded, and the interview was a nice opportunity to see how our interview protocols were working. The brewer showed us the brewing operation and discussed how things worked in the location as well as answering our questions about the craft beer community and ideas about craft beer, digital media, and the values of the craft beer economy. After the interview was more or less over, the three people sat down and each enjoyed a beer while discussing the traits of beer. At one point, the brewer asked the wife of the member of our research team how she liked her beer. She told him she really liked it. It was an amber ale that had a nice malty sweetness and good hop balance. The brewer looked at her with a slightly amused look on his face. After a pause, he said to her, "don't get me wrong, I am really glad you like the beer. But it is not what I was going for." He then proceeded to tell us that the yeast had stalled out. He was hoping for a much drier finished product, but as the yeast stopped working, the beer was sweeter than he intended.

This led to a discussion about what the craft brewer was seeking and how it was an art. At the same time, there is a business to run and a whole 15-barrel batch of beer cannot be discarded because it did not achieve the final form that would have really distinguished it as a distinctive beer. Simply, you can't throw it away, it's cost prohibitive. Beer customers, who are either brewers themselves or a craft connoisseur, will recognize this too when they are drinking a beer. A craft connoisseur might have sat at the bar and discussed how it was a nice malty amber ale, but not terribly distinctive. The customer would have liked the beer, but not given it an "A" rating. Most of the reviews of beers one sees on Beer Advocate, Rate Beer, and Untapped are pretty critical. It is hard to get a top rating. It's not that the consumer does not like the beer they are drinking at the moment, they just don't think it is superlative.

DOI: 10.4324/9781003109686-7

In the 2010s, as our research was getting started, a number of people in the social sciences rediscovered an essay by the philosopher Harry Frankfurt. The essay, *On Bullshit* was originally published in the Raritan Review. Princeton University Press revived the essay and reprinted it in a very small hardback book. Overall, Frankfurt had a different concern in the essay than we do here. For him, bullshit was a sign of indifference in the culture as it moved away from worrying about truth or falsehood. It was a sign of cultural decline in the face of an ambivalent relativism. But for us doing research on craft production, there was a brief moment in the beginning of the book where Frankfurt, trying to illustrate the importance of caring about quality, used a line from Longfellow about the 19th century craftsmen.

> Wittgenstein once said that the following bit of verse by Longfellow could serve him as a motto:
>
> > In the elder days of art
> > Builders wrought with greatest care
> > Each minute and unseen part,
> > For the Gods are everywhere.
>
> The point of these lines is clear. In the old days, craftsmen did not cut corners. They worked carefully, and they took care with every aspect of their work. Every part of the product was considered, and each was designed and made to be exactly as it should be. These craftsmen did not relax their thoughtful self-discipline even with respect to features of their work which would ordinarily not be visible. Although no one would notice if those features were not quite right, the craftsmen would be bothered by their consciences. So, nothing was swept under the rug. Or, one might perhaps also say, there was no bullshit.
>
> (Frankfurt, 2005, pp. 20–21)

Our brewer, who we were interviewing on that very cold December night, in the early days of the study was indeed Longfellow's craftsman. He knew that the beer was not perfect, and it bothered him. He did not think it was a bad beer. He knew that others would enjoy it and that gave him pleasure. He knew he was doing his job for the business; it would sell well, and all would be well. But he also knew, in that "unseen part" that there was a flaw. And working on that flaw would drive him to do better.

## Craft

Periodically, craft sees a revival in the heart of industrial and consumer capitalism. Sennett (2008) suggests that craft is always part of social life as doing and thinking are linked as part of the human condition. And indeed, many people are involved in craft in their own lives, whether painting the house, knitting gloves, making beer, making food, etc. And this is never really calculated as part of the economic activity of a nation. And while this is always ongoing, craft occasionally rises to a larger awareness as it becomes something like an art and is important to a segment of society as a set of aesthetic experiences. Certainly, beginning with the new food movement in California in the 1960s, craft in consumables like food, wine, coffee, cheese, and beer have been an important part of American society and that of many other nations too.

Perhaps we can see the roots of this movement in the mass production and mass consumption that fueled the economic growth of the post-WWII economy. Critical scholars have pointed out that capital accumulation tends to occur in particular moments, and these waves of accumulation involved both particular arrangements of space and particular arrangements of power, all of which are contradictorily related (Arrighi, 2005; Harvey, 2000; Lefebvre, 1991). WWII provided a unique opportunity for accumulation of profit for various industries, and also for the creation of a middle class and a consumer public – especially in the United States, Europe, and Japan, but also later in a number of other nations. The massive destruction of the war created a context where economies and markets needed to be rebuilt. Further, after the great depression, the free market ideology of the early part of the century was put aside for a more regulated economy (Aglietta, 1976; Harvey, 1989). These conditions set the stage for the creation of factories for the industrial production of consumer goods as we discussed in Chapter 4. Perhaps one of the best examples to see this growth is the rise of automobile culture. Cars became a measure of affluence, as most families were able to buy a car, but also maybe have a second car, and even later a third car. Durable goods were increasingly in range of most average-income people and consumables were marketed by brand to mass audiences. As we said in Chapter 3, people at this point had an electric refrigerator or two. Breweries moved to bottling and canning beer. And beer consumption moved from the local pub to the living room or den where adults in the family consumed beer around the color TV.

Again, as discussed earlier in the book, massification brought "the good life" to many people. And because the economy was in a stage of rapid growth, incomes were growing too. Piketty (2014) points out that companies were more willing to provide workers a small share of the profits of this growth to keep them working and not interrupt growth. This is not to say there were no labor struggles and strikes. But the overall effect of the two and a half decades after WWII was the increased affluence of many people and the building of a middle class in a number of societies. Mass consumption became the hallmark of this era. That mass consumption, one might say, led to a culture of mediocrity. Many beer critics, including famed beer critic Michael Jackson, have suggested that beer became blander and more watered down to appeal to the lowest common denominator. Light beer was perhaps the ultimate result of this tendency toward the lowest common denominator. Critics began to suggest that the era of mass consumption was not only one of blandness and mediocrity but also one of passivity as people sipped their light beer and watched TV with little interaction. Campbell (2005, p. 24), drawing on the work of Slater (1997), suggests that the model of the consumer of this era was that of the "dupe." Also during this moment of massification was the rise of the shopping mall. Ritzer (1999) calling these spaces "cathedrals of consumption" pointed to these large spaces that celebrated consumption as an ultimate concern. Ironically, these spaces were filled with the same or similar stores, products, and experiences, which, as Ritzer says, led to a real absence of meaning in this cultural world. In this world, consumers will seek to find and develop meaning.

More recent theorists of consumption see consumers as active producers of meaning in the process of consuming. Miller (2012) suggests that the consumer is always engaged in an active process of transformation of the meaning of objects. He suggested that in Trinidad, it was often not the producers (e.g., the Coca Cola company) who imposed their products on the consumer. But rather it was the creative work of Trinidadians who made a place for the production and hence created the market for Coke in Trinidad (Miller, 2012). Miller suggests this is always the case in capitalism, and to focus too heavily on productivism is to miss what is really going on in a consumer society. If this is true of consumerism in general, both craft production and consumption take this idea much further. In fact, craft beer consumers not only produce advertising and marketing and a social environment as we have suggested in earlier chapters, but many of them are also producers of beer themselves. They make beer, they are fans of beer, and they use more of their efforts to make more fans of beer too.

## Authenticity Again

In previous chapters, we have looked at authenticity to see it was one of the ways that craft brewers defined themselves in contrast to big beer. As such, it has been an important symbol. In this chapter, we want to think more about authenticity as a value. One way to look at the craft revival is to see it as a conscious act of resistance against the consistent compromises and mediocrity foisted upon the consumer market by large-scale producers (e.g., Bud and Mcdonald's). The spaces of consumption are small, more unique, and built to foster a kind of community through conversation and interaction. And the products produced in these spaces are to be celebrated, discussed, and consumed slowly. Craft production and consumption then is a resistance movement of a sort. And we can see parallel movements like the slow food movement beginning in the mid-1980s. Campbell (2005, p. 28) suggests that craft consumers "humanize" the product. Craft promises the possibility of meaning, but in that promise, it raises questions of authenticity. How do we know that an object is the product of craftsmanship, and thus has a real value, and not something that is a simulation of craft? And that threat of simulation is a way that instrumental goals are disguised as something else. In *The Ethics of Authenticity*, philosopher Charles Taylor suggests that one of the "malaises" of modern society is the rise and the priority of instrumental reason (Taylor, 1991, p. 8). In the 1990s, one of the first waves of craft was the production and sale of furniture, rugs, fabrics, and other household objects that semiotically indicated an indigenous and genuine production. But many of these objects were in fact mass produced. And the ones that were indeed produced by indigenous people were often people whose traditional way of life had been displaced and they were now doing piece work for the global economy, while being paid little money for the crafts they produced, and some large company was reaping the profit. The product was not only not authentic but disguised the exploitation in its production.

In craft beer, there were specific issues of authenticity that arose. The questions of craft were of course about where the product was made and was it legitimately craft production made by an independent producer. To this day, size is an important measure of a craft brewery. As we have said, the Brewer's association definition of craft, that we looked at earlier, included small size as one of the criteria. Over time, as breweries have grown, small size has had to be redefined. And indeed, size is a tension for the craft community. As breweries get bigger, their legitimacy becomes questioned. Can one authentically produce a craft product in a very large brewery? Often with scale comes the loss of location as breweries open up different large breweries in different parts of the country. Maintaining a commitment to the local community and being seen as a community member become more difficult. Further, with scale comes the problem of value that we will discuss in much more detail below. As maintaining a physical plant and supporting employees becomes more important, money and finances begin to be the most important things, as the crafting of the product becomes secondary to this larger pressure. In earlier chapters, we talked about New Belgium Brewery. We can see New Belgium as a paradigm of a brewery working on maintaining craft values while growing and finally being taken over by a global conglomerate. At each step, New Belgium has thought carefully about the issues of growth and how to remain true to its passion for values that are not traditionally part of the way a business might think about growth. New Belgium is a model when thinking about this idea of introducing more progressive ideas around the well-being of workers, the environment, and the quality of the product. It has shown that other values, besides profit, can be successfully maintained as an organization grows.

Craft beer also grew out of a history of brewers looking for beers with different flavor and a legitimation of these different recipes for beer. Many of the early craft brewers of the 1990s and 2000s grew up on American adjunct lagers that were produced by the very large breweries. These individuals were looking for more interesting flavors and brewing styles. Those early craft brewers, many of whom were former homebrewers, looked to Europe for the genuine styles of different kinds of interesting beer. And so, they looked to Belgium, France, Germany, England, Scotland, Ireland, and elsewhere for lagers and ales. These beers, because they came from different traditions, were very differentiable. They tasted different and were made of different ingredients. They were not all the same kind of adjunct lager. Further, they had histories and traditions behind them with some breweries dating back to the 14th and 15th centuries. And so, authenticity got defined around particular styles that came from specific locations, had specific histories, etc. Yeast manufacturers began to collect the house yeasts from many of Europe's famous breweries and began to cultivate strains of these yeasts for brewing either at the homebrew, or craft brewery level. As homebrewers and craft brewers began to brew beer from all these different traditions, formal bodies began to lay out the specific parameters for what defined a particular style. And so, a Belgian Saison had a specific color, flavor profile, alcohol content, etc. And these things defined the grains to be used as well as the hops, yeasts, and adjuncts. As craft is about quality, competitions arose for the best homebrewed and craft-brewed beers, and beers are judged according to standardized style guidelines such as those established by the Beer Judge Certification Program, Inc. (BJCP) style guidelines or the Brewers Association style guidelines. Beers that win in these competitions are ones that are excellent within the parameters of the style. This raises another interesting tension for brewers around authenticity. Brewers are very invested in these awards, they are important symbols of quality, excellence, and are a sign of value. As craftspersons, they care deeply about the recognition of their art. This is particularly important for a craft brewery that might attract a clientele based on their reputation for being excellent. Awards won are often placed on the beer can and prominently displayed in the brewery or brewpub.

At the same time, a tradition was in the process of being invented for craft beer around the various styles of beer one finds around the world, brewers were looking to be innovative. We have already talked about how West Coast IPAs pushed the bitterness profile of IPA. The traditional British IPA was hop forward, but a more balanced beer where a caramel malt sweetness was balanced with bittering hops. The West Coast style pushed that much further and IPAs of the late 90s and early 2000s had very high IBUs (International Bitterness Unit). That style reigned for a number of years, and there are still a number of very highly rated IPAs that are in the West Coast Style. Then a few years back, a new IPA style was developed that was called the New England IPA (NEIPA). New England IPAs were a cloudy beer. And cloudy used to be the sign of a failed beer when associated with an IPA. Further, NEIPAs had almost no bitterness. Many of them were brewed with no bittering hops and only flavor and aroma hops resulting in very low IBUs.[1] These beers were really "out of style" when they began, and it would have been difficult for them to win awards. In fact, many beer experts today still argue that the NEIPA should not be seen as an IPA at all but rather should be categorized as a New England Pale Ale. This is because they are so far from what has traditionally been an IPA. Innovation and creativity are also the mark of an excellent brewer(y). A truly innovative beer can be more important than an award winner. So, the tension between tradition and innovation pushes on the definition of authenticity in craft beer as well.

In any art, one must conform to standards and try to push the frontiers of that standard. It is a process of articulating that one has perfected the craft, but also has vision. So, beer is not alone in this process. And as it is a commercial product, like so many other crafts, this means that conforming to existing tastes is very important. Many of the tastes in craft beer that are popular today would have been unrecognizable as beer 40 years ago at the height of the popularity of adjunct lagers. Part of the tension between conforming to existing standards and innovation is about training an audience's taste but maintaining that audience's trust in the authenticity of the craftspersons. Craft breweries also specialize along this spectrum. Some are known to be "out there" with their sours, wild yeast beers, and beers that use unique grain and hop combinations. Some breweries are known to be very competent with traditional standards, the best stouts, saisons, etc.

Finally, there is the issue of selling out. As craft brewing has continued to grow, a number of breweries have now sold to "big beer," that is, one of the world's largest corporate conglomerates. Part of the definition of a craft brewery is its independence, the Brewer's Association defines independent as, "Less than 25 percent of the craft brewery is owned or controlled (or equivalent economic interest) by a beverage alcohol industry member that is not itself a craft brewer."[2] Previously, we talked about how New Belgium Brewery was not only a model of an excellent relationship between management and the workers, but it was also a model for how to sell to a big conglomerate, and maintain an ethical set of standards. And if New Belgium is a model for "selling out" and maintaining one's values, many other breweries are not seen by consumers and other brewers in such a positive light. If a brewery can no longer be seen as "craft" after selling more than 25% of the business, as that percentage goes up, often the status of the brewery goes down in the community. Literally the brewery starts to look bad to others in the craft beer community and there will be talk about how the quality of the beer has declined.[3] Independence, along with size, are probably the two most important boundary markers of craft. This is because selling out undermines the value that has been created in the process of being part of the craft community and independence and small size are a barricade to protect the value of craft beer.

## Value and Values

All these issues surrounding the questions of authenticity lead us to one of the main points of this chapter, and that is the question of value. Primarily, craft is about embracing a different set of values from those embraced by the companies engaged in mass production. We see that in the Longfellow quote at the beginning of the chapter. Craft is about being beholden to a higher power and shoddy workmanship cannot escape the eyes of the gods. Big beer is clearly not beholden to these higher values, and the argument would go, that is why they produce such a mediocre product (perhaps here mediocre means a product that does not have much meaning). So, craft holds a different set of values that can only be supported and maintained when the business is a small enough scale that one can keep one's eyes on all aspects of the craft, and where apprentices can carefully be trained into the community of practice. One must maintain one's distance from big beer, which is only beholden to profit, because undoubtedly big beer will sell out the values of quality, community, and balance.

An argument we make in this work is that the values of craft, and craft brewing, are also a form of "Value," the way economists might talk about economic value. This assertion raises the question of what is the relationship between value, as in economic value, and the values of a people, the things they really care about. Anthropologist Graeber (2001, 2013) has written extensively on this topic. Graeber suggests that this concern for the relationship between value and values has been a minor theme in the field of cultural anthropology. Graeber goes back to the work of Polanyi (1944), the political economist who wrote *The Great Transformation*, suggesting this work was one of the first efforts to link value to values.

In *The Great Transformation*, Polanyi suggests that there are two different kinds of economic systems in human societies. There are those societies with a formal economic sector, which is set off from the other institutions of society and where purely instrumental economic activity goes on. Then there are smaller scale societies with substantivist economies. Drawing on the ethnographic work of Bronislaw Malinowski, Polanyi suggests that in these societies, economic activity, such as raising pigs, is not separated from the other institutions of society. Rather, this economic activity is woven in the systems of kinship, religion, social organization, often through ritual and systems of reciprocal exchange. Further, the separation of the economy from these other institutions was itself a historical process and one that in the end separated large scale from small-scale societies.

Graeber points out that Polanyi raised these important questions about value and values, but the debate was never really settled. Except for a few researchers, Graeber suggests that this discussion was just more or less forgotten. When Graeber resurrects this discussion, he raises the most important question for us writing about craft beer (or anything craft of DIY) and, that is, what is value? Marx raised the same question albeit in a different way. Marx suggested in his work that human labor was the real value, human sensuous behavior. And what the capitalist successfully has done is a kind of sleight of hand by fetishizing the things that people produce. The capitalist suggests that it is the market that determines the value of things, and things are worth what people are willing to pay for them. This is Marx's labor theory of value, and it is the cornerstone of his work critiquing capitalist economics. As a number of researchers building on Marx have suggested, the capitalist economy depends on the reification of processes into things and a fetishistic belief that those things have power. So, money is ironically "the coin of the realm" and the market is the place where the transformation of value takes place. We don't see value as located in the labor that went into producing things as Marx would like, but rather in the things themselves.

But Marx, a good 19th century evolutionist, completely believed in the primacy of production, that production was, at least originally, organized around necessities, and the purpose of the good was given in the nature of reality, and so value could simply be expressed as the labor going into production. This 19th century materialist belief is also at the core of Marx's key concepts, use value and exchange value. Graeber shares with Marx an emphasis on human activity, but, like several critics of Marx, wants to also focus on the human preoccupation with meaning making through our activity. Drawing on the work of his mentors Munn (1986) and Turner (1979), Graeber suggests that value is produced with social groups and as Bourdieu has shown more recently, the individuals in particular social groups are engaged in a competition over status, as defined by that group. Munn's work focused on how human activity exists within what she called a space-time framework. The human activity in that frame was the way the people created meaning and value. Similarly, but working within a Marxist framework, Turner worked to redefine Marx's value as that activity that is central to human existence. We can certainly understand that if one did not live within a society that participated in the system of Kula exchange, one would not "feel" that Kula rituals and Kula objects were the most meaningful and important things in the world. One has to be part of that system and as a collective see this activity as the most important and meaningful activity (Graeber, 2001).

For example, Bourdieu (1988) showed that among academicians, the status game was one around the forms and use of cultural capital. And further, within that universe individuals occupy different positions in the status field as determined by their disciplines, the cultural capital they have accumulated in terms of status of degrees, publications, awards, etc. This game of status is very particular to academics and is unlike the kind of value creation that happens in the automobile or the finance industry, for example. The forms of value are different, and the activities are different. And yet, we can say that the game of status is played rather similarly. For that matter, we could say the same of the Kula exchange system in the Trobriand Islands.

This brings Graeber to suggest that it is value that is the measure in these different social worlds and that status competition is a competition for the highest forms of value. In the process of this productive activity, there are "products" that are the result of the activities that people are engaged in and that they value. As such, these products become "valuable" in themselves. The products are the tokens of the game. The activities the people engage in and the products of that activity, including the social media products, are all symbolic. This leads Graeber, drawing on Weber, to another theoretical point. He suggests the participants in a particular "field" of activity, to borrow Bourdieu's term, are not only trying to accumulate status within their field, but they are attempting to make their game the most important game in the society (Graeber, 2013, pp. 227–228).

Moving back to craft beer, we can see that much of what we have been talking about around craft, quality, authenticity, and innovation is really about the game of status that occurs within the homebrewing and craft brewing communities. This is also why beer competitions are so important. Brewers compete to make the best beers as defined by well-crafted quality, interesting taste, and innovative ideas. In this, great beers are valued, new styles of beer are valued, as is careful attention to detail. For Bourdieu, this is a social field where this game goes on and rules and strategies evolve as the brewing community evolves. Craft fans and consumers can participate in this game too. Just as the beer produced reflects the human social relationships and the status game that brewers play, out of this, consumers can buy high-status beers. Fans themselves garner status points by being able to say they have had high-status beers that might be out of one's geographic area and hard to get such as Pliny the Younger or Heady Topper. Below we will talk more about beer cans and the labels on them as a marker of this status potential for fans. Further, the knowledge of what is the latest most important beer, where it comes from, how it was made, can make one a trend setter as a consumer.

Bourdieu (1990) was something of a quantum sociologist, in that he understood how there were overlapping fields of activity where a different levels of game play went on. So, there is also a larger field of beer competition where craft brewers struggle with large corporate brewers over control of what is valued in beer. And this competition is not about beer competitions where brewers compete to brew the best IPA. This competition is over larger values and control of the beer market. As such, large brewers historically worked to maintain control of the distribution systems. And craft brewers competed with the market to show consumers that the values of taste, quality, and innovation were more important than easy drinking and mass market appeal. The idea of status competitions explains why big beer was so concerned with the growth of craft beer. To this day, craft beer only controls 12.3% of the beer market by volume.[4] But at the same time, until the pandemic began, and for about a decade, craft beer was the only segment of the market that was growing. So, in terms of the status game, craft beer was winning. Graeber points out that for his mentor Terence Turner, the ability to control which status game is the most important game in town is in fact determined by politics, and so we could say that all economics is political too (Graeber, 2013, p. 228a).

Further, what is important to us, as researchers concerned with the commodification of social life, in this struggle over value, is that the craft beer community valued things that were what Durkheim or Merton might call pro-social. Craft beer values community, and locally produced products, and fair wages for workers. The craft beer community is concerned with the environment and thinks about how beer depends on quality ingredients and a healthy environment. And as we have said before, while making money is an important part of any business, money making is not "ultimate" in the craft beer community. Craft, and social well-being are the ultimate concerns. So, the struggle with big beer is over what we value in beer, but it is also a struggle for much more, it's a struggle against the mass market commodified life and a move toward a more human scale and a concern for things that are good for all people. Of course, this is not just craft beer, one finds these values in any community that might call itself "craft."

## Beer Labels

There are volumes and volumes written on beer labels. Entire books discuss design and fonts, others catalog history, and others focus on iconography and symbology. There is far too much on the subject to do justice to here. But let us take a superficial stab at it.

Craft brewers are typically at a serious disadvantage in terms of marketing reach and resources. The big breweries can out-produce, out-distribute, out-promote, and out-display any of the beers they produce. This is just another advantage of big beer's deep pockets. One of the ways craft producers have found the space to stand out in a crowded marketplace is to have distinctive and engaging labeling. Today craft beer labels run the gamut in terms of stylistic approaches. Some are works of art, some amusing visuals or jokes, some are takes on iconic and classic labels, others works of brilliant minimalism, and still others pop culture references or in-jokes, and there are even those that defy categorization. While all these labels make their beers distinctive on the shelf, it should be said that this drive for uniqueness in appearance began partially due to market expectations of product appearance, but the innovations craft brewers made were equally due to the limitations they faced when it came to designing their labels and physically getting them on the cans and bottles.

In a similar way, Cavanaugh (2019) talks about artisanal cheese makers in Italy, and the way they label their cheeses to make the authenticity of the cheese stand out. Like craft brewers, artisanal cheese makers do not have access to a big marketing budget, or sophisticated equipment to make signs to label their cheese. So, they have taken to handwritten, very clearly non-professional labels. The semiotic of these labels, like the creative non-professional labels of craft beers, makes them stand out and signals to a consuming public that this product is authentically craft (Cavanaugh & Shankar, 2014). In both cases, the artisanal producers of beer and cheese turn a disadvantage into an advantage. Of course, the large producers then turn around and create mass market versions of these handmade labels. This becomes a form of status consumption around signs. We have already seen in Chapter 6 that signs, such as posts in social media, are themselves a form of value and an important part of the overlap between production and consumption.

Historically, beer labels have been a paper label on a glass bottle. By the late-1950s, printing labels directly onto cans became the popular choice for breweries canning beer. Later shrink-wrapping labels around cans became a popular option. By the beginning of the craft beer revolution, all of the major breweries were literally and figuratively invested in these labeling styles. They owned the labeling machines. And their brands, the look and feel of their bottles and cans, were known commodities. The big breweries saw no reason to spend money to deviate from what they were doing. But this approach allowed for creative and innovative craft brewers to find space in the crowded beer market by making their product appear different enough to stand out on the shelves and in the coolers.

The early days of craft beer labeling generally followed the trends of the major producers as they existed at the time. Labels depicted stylized names and logos (e.g., early Dogfish Head labels), and iconography classically associated with beer. Think here of men hoisting steins (e.g., Rogue labels) or a logo wrapped in hops and barley (e.g., Anchor Steam) or bucolic nature scenes (e.g., Sierra Nevada). But as more craft producers entered the market, using labels that could get lost among those already out there seemed like an injudicious approach. New breweries introduced new approaches to label designs, new concepts for what labels and logos could look like, and especially as canning became common for craft brewers thanks to rental canning lines, what materials labels were made of.

The advent of rental canning lines that traveled to small craft breweries and canned and labeled their product for them is the material shift that really spurred the craft beer label transformation forward. The technological shift was that these canning lines allowed brewers to fill blank cans, clean any spilled beer from them with a spray of water on the canning line, and move to the label application process while the can was still wet, crucially skipping the drying step needed for can printing, reducing energy consumption, and expediting the process. Thanks to moisture-resistant adhesives and waterproof foil labels, the process is fairly cheap, easy once the canning line is in place, and allows for labels of any design to easily be put on cans. Many modern labels have a high-quality textured feel. The effect of this is that labeling became a more dynamic process. Certainly, flagship beers had their labels remain constant, but breweries also started experimental series, and barrel-aged series where the beer and the label changed throughout the series. Labels were becoming almost as important to the consumption process as the beer was. Artists and graphic designers were hired. Great care and effort were taken with label design and production. Everything about them being seriously considered. Some breweries began to make their labels collectors' items, making them high-quality removable stickers. Some went as far as making all of the labels in a particular series fit together to form a poster or a piece of art. All of this served to make each brewery unique in their design within the market, but it also served to distinguish craft breweries in general from big beer. One brewer we interviewed said this regarding how they think about label design, "Well, we have versatility and we're not trying to turn around a massive juggernaut. For us to do something different we can be quite dynamic. We can do that in a matter of weeks. For them [big breweries] to do something dynamic…It's a whole production." What this brewer meant is obvious. The big breweries are beholden to their owned, tried-and-true labeling systems, with their paper labels and printed or shrink-wrapped cans. As with quality and flavor so in labeling, the space the big beers forgot about or overlooked is where the craft beers thrived and created their niche. The ability of small breweries to be nimble and produce unique artistic labels for small batches is perhaps an analogue to the handmade signs of the Italian cheese makers. The added advantage for craft beer is that this move is not quite so easily simulated by big beer.

We see here with labels, another form of value creation. Craft brewers and consumers see these labels as forms of value themselves. Individuals and homebrew shops have trophy cases of unique labels displayed, especially if the beers are hard to get. This symbolic activity is another way to add to the value being produced in the community.

## From Being to Becoming

In *Being and Time*, Heidegger (1927/1962) suggests that there is an essential contradiction for human beings (Dasein). Human beings are free and driven to become, to create something new. Yet at the same time one is part of a world, and that world provides the very frame of practice and meaning within which people operate. And so, the creative energy gets caught up in the forces of the everyday. Spinosa, Flores, and Dreyfus (1997) use this Heideggerian framework to talk about the ways that entrepreneurs and people engaged in democratic action and solidarity movements are different from other people. They refer to the entrepreneurial process as one of "disclosing new worlds."

Like Heidegger's notion of the "world," Spinosa, Flores, and Dreyfus talk about a disclosive space. And like Heidegger, a disclosive space is a space where practices, tools, intentions, and identities are all coordinated to achieve specific goals. Certainly, beer production could be such a disclosive space. And as such it would involve the tools and technologies to produce beer, the intentions and practices, and the identities as brewer all folded into a particular world. Spinosa, Flores, and Dreyfus suggest that in any disclosive space, the regular practices that people engage in, and the ways they go about these practices and the tools they use inevitably produce certain tensions. They refer to these tensions as "disharmonies" (Spinosa et al., 1997, p. 22). Disharmonies exist in every disclosive space, but they are often not recognized as such. Spinosa, Flores, and Dreyfus suggest this is because the things we encounter in our world are not just things, but they are meaningful things and activities. And as such meaningful things fit together to make the disclosive space understandable, it is familiar. It is part of our lives, it is the "water we swim in" so to speak. Spinosa, Flores, and Dreyfus refer to "style" as the way things fit together in a disclosive space such that all is coordinated (Spinosa et al., 1997, p. 19). Because this is all a meaningful whole, we tend to overlook disharmonies within that space.

Entrepreneurs are people who not only notice the disharmony, but they also focus on it. Unlike the ordinary citizen, they continue to struggle with disharmonies. As they reflect on disharmonies, they begin to think about whether this is a personal tension, or one that is shared with others. And as they think about how this world produces disharmony for themselves and others, they begin to imagine ways to reconfigure the style, the way the world fits together. This might involve drawing on new tools or resources from other arenas of life that could be brought into this disclosive space. As they begin this innovative process, the whole disclosive space will shift. The world as it was will no longer be the same. It's easy to pick an example like smartphones to see how this is the case. The world after smartphones is not the same world as the one before they existed.

If we think about craft brewers and the kind of entrepreneurs that Spinosa, Flores, and Dreyfus talk about, we can see how their model helps us understand the craft-brewing world. There were several disharmonies that existed in the world of beer before craft. Joe Ortlieb, the owner of the family business Ortlieb's beer, one of the last of the Philadelphia breweries before the craft revolution, was rumored to complain about how national beer, and light beer were products with just more water. We have already seen how beer expert Michael Jackson said that big beer was really a mediocre product. One disharmony was that the mass consumer movement of the post-WWII era had led to a bland and uninteresting product. Several of the brewer/owners we talked to, talked about pursuing beers with more interesting flavors. But mass consumption had led also to other forms of alienation. Beer, once a community activity, was now an individual, private experience. It was no longer connected to the community or the environment we all live in. This disharmony was not unique to beer of course and the response to this disharmony on the part of many entrepreneurs fueled the craft food, bread, wine, and coffee movements as well. It was this set of disharmonies that the craft-brewing entrepreneurs began to focus on and set out to change. And in the process, they transformed the disclosive space.

A central part of that transformation was that the focus was not just on making money, but really dealing with these disharmonies that were more about alienation and quality of life. In *The Ethics of Authenticity*, Taylor (1991) suggests that there are several "malaises" of our era. The two main ones Taylor focuses on is the rise of individualism and the priority of instrumental reason over other systems of value. Taylor has a larger political concern as these forces are producing a world where it is harder to argue for larger moral concerns like the environment because these concerns are drowned out by the preoccupation with the satisfaction of the individual and rational calculation. But in the same way, craft beer entrepreneurs raise the question of quality of life, community, people's social well-being, and other forms of value that are as important as making money and having a successful business. Going back to Graeber, in this way, these entrepreneurs challenge the dominant "game" in contemporary societies of making profit. And it is this challenge that makes studying the craft beer movement, as well as other craft moments, important.

At the same time, this challenge is contradictory and exists within a context of pressures that press for the failure of raising these other forms of value to being the dominant activity and hence form of value. We have already seen how craft beer found a niche because of the transformations in the spatial arrangement of global capitalism and the transformation of cities from industrial wastelands into thriving urban centers of an information age. It is in the gentrified neighborhoods and among the tastes of the new successful middle class that craft beer found its audience. Further, as some of the craft breweries of the 1990s see a lot of success, they must face the pressures of growth and the need to prioritize finance and growth.

## Conclusion

In the 2010s, as craft beer was experiencing very rapid growth both in terms of volume of sales and income, it was not uncommon to see articles about how craft breweries were focused more on collaboration and not competition. We could think about the period from 2010 to 2018 as a period of the greatest growth in craft beer, and on the one hand there was so much beer and money to be made, it was easy for breweries to focus on collaboration and not competition. Further, craft beer had come out of a period where they had struggled against big beer and a need for knowledge and materials to succeed. So, craft breweries needed each other. But further, collaboration not competition helped reinforce a social imaginary for brewers, owners, and consumers that craft beer was different. It was different from big beer and from other industries. And it was an example of a more human kind of business, where workers were treated better, owners sought the best possible products and social environments, and the business cared about the larger community and larger social issues. In Taylor's terms, they were "authentic" ventures.

We see a genuine value in this utopian moment. Somewhat at odds with the larger capitalist economy in their struggle against big beer, craft beer can be seen as a model for alternative forms of economic development that don't just focus on financial growth but consider quality of life as a measurable value. And while this may seem like a small thing, craft practices do provide a model for living differently and embracing a different set of values. At the same time that this was a utopian moment, and perhaps one that has already passed, craft beer grew out of a hobby shared by largely middle-class white men. And recently we have become very aware of the struggles of women and people of color in this movement. So, given that craft beer depended on evolution of the consumer culture within global capitalism, as well as being structured around existing systems of inequality, we can see that the moment was indeed very contradictory. It is to some of those contradictions that we turn to in the next chapter.

## Notes

1 Bittering hops have a higher alpha acid content that lends bitterness to beer. Alpha Acids are the active part of the resin of the hop cone. Further, that bitterness in hops is released when the wort (the liquid combination of water and malt sugars) is boiled. The typical boil time for a beer is 60 minutes, sometimes 90 minutes. In general, the earlier in the boil that hops are added, the more bitterness they contribute to the beer. And hops with higher alpha acid added earliest in the wort, often the 60-minute mark, create the most bitterness. Many NEIPAs only add hops after the fire has been turned off and the boil is finished. This way, they can add flavor and aroma, but no bitterness.
2 https://www.brewersassociation.org/statistics-and-data/craft-brewer-definition/
3 In 1990, Dorothy Holland and Margaret Eisenhardt published a study, *Educated in Romance: Women, Achievement, and College Culture.* In this book, one of the central findings was that men's status in the university was linked to their institutional positions, for example, being on the football team, in a fraternity, etc. Women's status, however, was linked to their ability to attract high status men, either as boyfriends, or a participant in activities that women were organizing such as fundraisers. When a woman broke up with a high-status male, the community would say that she lost beauty. There would be comments that she was not looking good. Beauty was a marker of her status. In a parallel way, when an independent craft brewery links to big beer, that brewery loses some or all its "beauty." Status of the brewery is inversely related to how close the brewery is to big beer.
4 For these and other statistics see: https://www.brewersassociation.org/statistics-and-data/national-beer-stats/s

## References

Aglietta, M. (1976). *A theory of capitalist regulation: The US experience.* London: Verso.

Arrighi, G. (2005). Hegemony unraveling - 2. *New Left Review,* (33), 83–116.

Bourdieu, P. (1988). *Homo academicus.* Stanford, CA: Stanford University Press.

Bourdieu, P. (1990). *The logic of practice.* Stanford, CA: Stanford University Press.

Campbell, C. (2005). The craft consumer: Culture, craft and consumption in a postmodern society. *Journal of Consumer Culture, 5*(1), 23–42. https://doi.org/10.1177/1469540505049843

Cavanaugh, J. R. (2019). Labeling authenticity, or, how I almost got arrested in an Italian supermarket. *Semiotic Review,* 5. https://semioticreview.com/ojs/index.php/sr/article/view/47

Cavanaugh, J. R., & Shankar, S. (2014). Producing authenticity in global capitalism: Language, materiality, and value. *American Anthropologist, 166*(1), 51–64.

Frankfurt, H. (2005). *On bullshit.* Princeton, NJ: Princeton University Press.
Graeber, D. (2001). *Toward an anthropological theory of value: The false coin of our own dreams.* New York, NY: Palgrave Macmillan.
Graeber, D. (2013). It is value that brings universes into being. *HAU: Journal of Ethnographic Theory, 3*(2), 219–243.
Harvey, D. (1989). *The conditions of postmodernity.* Oxford: Basil Blackwell.
Harvey, D. (2000). *Spaces of hope.* Berkeley, CA: University of California Press.
Heidegger, M. (1962). *Being and time.* New York, NY: Harper and Row. (Original work published 1927).
Lefebvre, H. (1991). *The production of space.* Oxford: Basil Blackwell.
Miller, D. (2012). *Consumption and its consequences.* Cambridge: Polity Press.
Munn, N. (1986). *The fame of Gawa: A symbolic study of value transformation in a Massim (Papua New Guinea) society.* Cambridge: Cambridge University Press.
Piketty, T. (2014). *Capital in the twenty-first century.* (A. Goldhammer, Trans.). London; Cambridge, MA: Belknap Press of Harvard University.
Polanyi, K. (1944). *The great transformation: The political and economic origins of our time.* Boston, MA: Beacon Press.
Ritzer, G. (1999). *Enchanting a disenchanted world: Revolutionizing the means of consumption.* Thousand Oaks, CA: Pine Forge Press.
Sennett, R. (2008). *The craftsman.* New Haven, CT: Yale University Press.
Slater, D. (1997). *Consumer culture & modernity.* Cambridge: Polity Press in association with Blackwell Publishing.
Spinosa, C., Flores, F., & Dreyfus, H. L. (1997). *Disclosing new worlds: Entrepreneurship, democratic action, and the cultivation of solidarity.* Cambridge, MA: MIT Press.
Taylor, C. (1991). *The ethics of authenticity.* Cambridge, MA: Harvard University Press.
Turner, T. (1979). Anthropology and the politics of indigenous peoples' struggles. *Cambridge Anthropology, 5*, 1–43.

# 8 Blurring the Edges

## Craft Beer's Limitations

### Introduction

As we have discussed at several points in this volume, we got interested in craft beer for three main reasons. First and most importantly, this was an industry that was growing rapidly and one that embraced a set of values that challenged the dominant instrumental value of making money. And again, as we have said several times, making money is of course important for any new venture. And the early craft breweries really struggled with making enough money to stay afloat. But as the 1990s shifted to the 2000s, and the industry experienced rapid growth, the values of taste and quality, community, environment, just treatment of workers, collaboration and not competition, became as important as making money. This was a real counterpoint to the normal principles of capitalist practice. And in the era of neoliberalism, where "commodification" was the watchword of other kinds of industries going the other way – that is making profit more important than other human values – craft beer was an interesting phenomenon. We were aware that we were studying craft beer at perhaps a utopian moment, but the fact that an industry could do well and engage in more humane and pro-social values made it important to think about, even if it were only a moment.

The second reason we were very interested in craft beer was the dependence of the industry and individual ventures on digital media. We have argued that without the internet and the evolution of social media, it would have been very hard for craft beer ventures to succeed at the small scale where many breweries and brewpubs started. Digital media also made craft beer a community where the lines of production and consumption were blurred, and all involved felt they were part of the phenomenon. The third reason for our interest was connected to the second, digital media helped create the phenomenon of prosumption where the lines between producer and consumer were blurred. Media posts on the part of consumers were themselves a form of work.

We, therefore, were not focused on some of the other challenges of the industry. When we first began this work, it was very clear that this was a very white and male world. We were somewhat happy to see that just

DOI: 10.4324/9781003109686-8

anecdotally it looked like the craft movement had led to many more women craft beer consumers. And indeed Bart Watson, economist for the Brewers Association, suggests that women, especially young women, are an increasing percentage of the craft beer consumers.[1] But at the time of our study, there was very little diversity among the producers and consumers of craft beer. In this chapter, we will be looking into that lack of diversity.

We also became aware of the challenge of the overuse of alcohol through our research. While this should not have surprised us, it was not a focus when we started. We slowly began to see the ways the over consumption of alcohol was very much part of the culture of craft beer. And this is true among craft brewers, homebrewers, and the fans of craft beer. In his famous study of working class "lads" in Britain, sociologist Willis (1981) talked about the ways that these "bad boys" of the school saw through the class system and were very critical of the ways the system was not going to give them a chance to get ahead. But at the same time, there were limitations to their consciousness, and Willis demonstrates how their view of women and other students of color limited their critique of the social system, and drove them to choose a future of a limited horizon. In a loose parallel way, we see the racism, sexism, and alcoholism in the craft beer community as a real limiting counterpoint to the exciting way this industry demonstrates an alternative set of values.

## Craft Beer and Alcoholism

Early on in our research, we went to a tap takeover in a craft beer bar. The bar was located in a popular suburb. Tap takeovers were at that point relatively novel events. They were posted on websites and in social media. They offered consumers an opportunity to taste the beers from a particular brewery. They also offered the fan of craft beer an opportunity to meet people from the brewery and have a conversation. Sometimes head brewers would come to the takeover, and sometimes the owner and other members of the team would come too. For fans, there was the potential of gaining status in the community as you posted pictures of yourself buying beers at the event with brewery personnel. For the brewery, this was a great form of inexpensive advertising and an example of the prosumption we have talked about in previous chapters. Simply by organizing a few kegs of their beer with the bar, and some time from brewery personnel, a lot of buzz could be generated as people posted to Twitter, Instagram, Facebook, and other media sites. The status of the pub was also improved with these tap takeovers as they became seen as a center in the craft beer movement.

On this particular rainy evening, the owner and the marketing representative were both at this tap take over. The owner, and original brewer was a man, the marketing rep was a woman, a gender makeup we saw a lot and part of what we will talk about in the next section. Both were white as were most of the customers in the bar, and we will talk about race in the last section of the chapter. The brewery was from another state. It went from a small brewpub to a larger scale brewery (although still small) and was looking to break into the Philadelphia market. Over the course of the evening, we had a very good conversation with the marketing rep. She was busy supporting the bar, but also was able to stop and talk with us a number of times. The owner had a lot of fans around him and was being kept very busy. As the night wore on, we could see that the owner was becoming pretty intoxicated. In fact, the festival atmosphere led to a number of people in the bar getting very intoxicated. This is the first time that we focused on the question of the amount of drinking going on, and how the atmosphere supported the over consumption of beer. If this were a festival, you might say, oh well, a little overindulgence on a special night. But tap takeovers were becoming quite common. It's hard to take much more away from this story other than we wondered about the drinking habits of people in the industry, as well as the consumers.

In 2019, anthropologist and craft brewer Delgaty (2019) presented a paper at the American Anthropological Association annual meeting. Delgaty is in the unique position of being an industry insider as well as being trained as a cultural anthropologist. His ethnographic work gave him a more intimate view of a craft beer brewery than we were able to get. For Delgaty, there are three main pressures on brewers that press for the overconsumption of alcohol. First, beer is a perk of the job. Brewers are often able to have free drinks after a shift or even as a break during the day. Some breweries provide workers with an allotment of beer per month to take home. Beer is an easy perk to provide workers, because if a batch goes well and ferments properly, the per pint cost to the brewery is relatively low. Brewers are often invited to events where brewers from different breweries taste each other's beers and discuss the process and results. In these events, it is anti-social to not taste the beers that are on tap for discussion. Further, to leave a beer unfinished might be a comment on how the brewer did not like the beer. Events like these pressure individuals to drink perhaps more than they would want to.

Finally, beer production is anxiety producing. A 15–30 barrel batch of beer costs a brewery a significant amount of money to produce. And many things can go wrong. Brewers jokingly say that brewing is 90% cleaning. That is because after the boiling process is over, every piece of equipment that touches the boiled wort needs to be sterilized. Fermentation takes place in tanks that are not only sterile but sealed off from outside air by putting a blow off tube into a bucket of sanitizer. The fermentation process produces $CO_2$ that must be "blown off." And so, the blow off tube carries the $CO_2$ down to a bucket of liquid sterilizing fluid (the same liquid that bartenders use to clean glasses at the bar) where it safely bubbles out into the air but does not allow any air with bacteria and wild yeasts to get back into the fermenter. Keeping a batch of fermenting beer sterile is not the only issue. The yeast colony can stop eating sugar for some reason and one gets a stalled batch. Things can go wrong in the mash, and the boil, the earlier processes before fermenting. There are so many things that could go wrong. Some of those things, like the story we told in Chapter 7 where the beer ended up being sweeter than the brewer wanted, are disappointments to the brewer, but the beer can still be sold. Sometimes, when things go really wrong, a whole batch of beer must be thrown out. Delgaty suggests one of the ways that brewers cope with this anxiety is to drink. And since beer is right there and free, it is an easy way to self-medicate around the anxiety of brewing.

One interview we had with a local brewer is a little more indirect evidence. We were invited to the bar at the brewpub where the brewer worked. We met the brewer at the end of the day, around 5 p.m. It was a very nice warm late afternoon as we sat in the bar. We were offered a beer, and we, knowing the cultural rules, accepted and shared a beer with the brewer as he answered our questions and told us about the brewery. Over the course of the interview, the brewer had three beers. We were offered a second beer, but we politely declined. That might have been a little bit of a violation, or maybe a better way to put it is that we indicated, by our declining a second pint, that we came from a different culture. When the interview was over, we thanked the brewer and left him at the bar as he was considering whether to have a fourth pint. Four pints is not a lot in the minds of brewers. We have been to homebrew club meetings where brewers might drink a similar number of pints and not really consider that a big drinking evening. And, of course, the number of pints is just part of the calculation. A lot of craft beers are "higher gravity" as people in the culture would say, meaning that they have a higher alcohol by volume (ABV) than the traditional 4–5% of American adjunct lagers such as Miller High Life at 4.6% or Budweiser at 5%. In this story, it is again hard to know, did the brewer drink more than he would on another day because he was meeting us, and it was a social event? Or was it a stressful day as he worried over a batch of beer?

Craft beer consumers have not escaped this tendency to consume high ABV (alcohol by volume) beers. While research tends to indicate that overall beer consumption is down nationwide, it is also evident that people are drinking more high ABV beers than before. Anecdotally, from our research it looks like the fans of craft beer are drinking more beer and higher ABV beers. Certainly, we have seen this in our observations of home brew clubs. But to think about how large a percentage of the public this is, and whether craft beer is having any specific effect on alcohol use in the population, I don't think anyone can say at this point. And certainly, that would not be our point. What does seem to be quite clear among brewery insiders and close fans of craft beer is that drinking multiple pints of higher gravity beers is pretty normal.

## White Male Culture of Homebrewing and Craft Brewing

As we discussed early in the book, homebrewing was our entry point into the craft beer community. While neither of us as researchers were able to work in the industry and engage in participant observation that way, homebrewing allowed the study to move from an interview study to one that was more ethnographic. When we first started to attend homebrew club meetings, we were surprised by the way they looked like the images of popular science clubs of the 1960s. It was not just a white male culture, but it was a particular kind of "nerd" culture that one might find in the computer club, engineer club, or science club of the past. Homebrewers were not only mostly white and male, but they were very much into the crafting of their own equipment as well as crafting beer.

Homebrew clubs were very involved in the making of homemade mash tuns where the sugars are extracted from the grains. They made stir plates for creating a yeast starter by using a cigar box and the fan from an old computer. Beyond these homemade tools, homebrew club meetings were often about the chemistry of beer, the microbiology of beer, souring beers, etc. They were often about very mechanical and scientific aspects of beer. And we have seen before how these themes are part of the educational project of the National Homebrewing Association annual meeting, Homebrew Con.

Club meetings were often in breweries and brewery staff were often very active in bringing their perspective to these topics. While there is nothing particularly natural to these topics being of greater interest to white males, it is the case that most of the individuals attending and participating were white and male. Many of them were from scientific or engineering industries and backgrounds that were more white and male as well. When we first started attending homebrew club meetings, the few women who were there were partners of the men. And some of them were very interested in beer too. Over the time of our research, more women, unattached to men, were active members of the homebrew clubs. And in a few instances, the women were the main brewers, and their male partners were the ones who came along. So, over the period of our research, the gender makeup of these meetings shifted a bit. Racially, the groups were still almost exclusively white. We only participated in a few homebrew clubs, so one cannot make generalizations from that experience. The larger data set does show some change, but more or less lines up with what we were seeing.

## Craft Beer and Race

In a 2015 article in Thrillist magazine, author Dave Infante (2015) set out to figure out why there are no Black people brewing craft beer. He starts the article by talking about the beer bar he is in and how white the scene is. He goes on to point out that craft beer is whiter than many institutions that we consider very white institutions and activities, and he wonders why that is. He comes up with several main points of analysis that he thinks explains what he was seeing in 2015. First, he points out that Black people don't drink craft beer. In 2015, they consumed only 3.7% of the craft beer produced. That number has not changed much since 2015. And while there are some demographic shifts in craft beer consumption, the consumption on the part of people of color has only gone up slightly. From the perspective of craft beer consumption, craft beer is very overwhelmingly white.

Infante then goes on to informally investigate why Black people don't drink craft beer by interviewing a few of his colleagues. In general, people told him that craft beer was dominated by white culture and there were several reasons people did not want to participate in that scene. Infante's colleagues felt they were not welcome in the space. They also felt like they would get a lecture if they chose a regular beer. The image of the bearded, flannel shirted, hipster white male was off putting for people. This is not surprising. A quick review of the covers of Beer Advocate magazine reveals a recurring theme, the cover was a picture of one or several bearded white males in jeans and flannel. Beer Advocate, still a major website for craft beer, had a print magazine from 2007 to 2019. And, of course, over that period of time there were many different covers on the magazine. But, especially in the 20 teens, the bearded hipster white male was a regular feature of the cover art. And Beer Advocate was certainly not alone, other more local magazines had the same kinds of images that showed a very white culture.

While Infante says he did not encounter overt racism in craft beer, the fact that craft beer is overwhelmingly white is because beer is overwhelmingly white, and there is a long history of racism in beer. Taking a critical race theory perspective, Chapman and Brunsma (2020) point out in their book *Beer and Racism* that the United States has always been dominated by white supremacy. As such, the ideology of white privilege has structured all the institutions in the society and across time. They provide an excellent and detailed history of the ways that racism has been part of the organizations of local communities, and how breweries were part of more privileged and usually white communities. They point out that taverns were common in colonial America. These institutions were very much modeled on English and European institutions. They were part of white communities. Further, they go on to point out that as the tavern was a place where working people could engage in behavior that might not be in the interests of elites, elites were very concerned to regulate behavior. For them, this is one of the ways these become white spaces as the behavior within them are determined by white norms including who could be included and excluded (Chapman & Brunsma, 2020, pp. 36–37).

Infante focuses on prohibition and the post-prohibition era. Citing a conversation with J. Nikol Beckham, who at the time was at Randolph College, but now leads the Brewers Association's Diversity, Equity & Inclusion (DEI) department as the association's Equity & Inclusion Partner, he points out that the temperance movement used racist imagery to demonize drinking. And so, people of color and their behavior became the stereotype for what went on in a pub. In the post-prohibition era, as we pointed out in our history chapter, the beer industry was rapidly consolidating. And as beer became big, it also became part of the corporate mainstream in the American society. So again, white supremacy was operating, these were white institutions while the executives in those institutions may not have thought about it that way.

This history of white community control, racism, and elite corporate consolidation meant that overall, the brewing industry was a very white space, even as young craft brewers come into that space and are not necessarily aware of the role of race in that history. Early craft brewers were almost exclusively white, and they saw their battles as being more about the culture and interests of big beer versus the craft of craft beer. Race was excluded from the discourse. Chapman and Brunsma (2020, p. 53) point out that while the early homebrewers and craft brewers were reacting to big beer, they themselves were products of the same racist history that differentially distributed knowledge about brewing and the connections needed to brew, as well as capital needed to start a brewery. Many of the early brewers were not very affluent and had to put together money through loans from friends, lines of credit, and knowledge of cheap equipment and property. While this indeed was a struggle for many craft brewers, it still showed that they had both economic and cultural capital to draw on to get an entrepreneurial enterprise going. And that access was part of their white privilege even as it felt less like a privilege and more like a struggle.

Things, however, are slowly beginning to change. The Brewer's Association has taken a real interest in diversifying the industry and supporting owners and brewers of color. They established a diversity committee and have supported DEI initiatives. An example from our research, we regularly attended a beer tasting event at one of the homebrew shops in the Philadelphia area. These tastings have stopped for now due to COVID. But when they were going on, they happened at this shop about once every six weeks or so. The tastings were similar to a tasting event that would be part of a homebrew club meeting. And in fact, many of the attendees of the shop's tastings were members of local homebrew clubs. The shop owner himself was active in two of the homebrew clubs. At these events, people would bring samples of beers they had brewed recently. People would have small cups and serve an ounce or so of a beer to taste it and then talk with others about the beer. This was like a very informal critique one might see in an art studio where people would share successes, problems, techniques, etc. Two of the regular attendees of these tastings would always bring beers they were developing for the craft beer brewery they were planning on opening. They opened the brewery and pub in December of 2019. The brewery and pub are located in a majority black neighborhood in Philadelphia. The demographic makeup of the overall community as of the 2010 U.S. Census is 77% black, 15% white, 3% non-white Hispanic, and 2% Asian. The owners themselves are white. They are committed to diversity on a number of levels and their staff is very racially and gender diverse. It is one of the few small breweries in the Philadelphia area that has a truly diverse staff and a fairly diverse clientele. The brewery had to close again almost immediately due to the first wave of COVID restrictions, but the owners are very creative. They pivoted quickly to a canning operation and began taking orders and delivering beer in the Philadelphia area. Like a lot of restaurants and pubs, they developed a fairly large outdoor area in their large parking lot. It has become a lively and thriving institution in a diverse, fairly poor community.

After we officially stopped collecting data, there has been a buzz around the creation of Black-owned breweries. There are now an increasing number of Black-owned breweries getting started. Currently, Philadelphia has one Black-owned brewery. It was started by two brothers. Like so many brewers, they began homebrewing and they have slowly been moving toward a production brewery. Right now, they are looking for a space for the brewery. In the meantime, they are brewing some beers that are gaining real attention. They are available for pick-up and delivery, and they also show up at farmers markets and other spaces. In nearby Harrisburg, three Philadelphia natives are also in the planning stages of what they call Pennsylvania's first Black-owned brewery. A 2019 article in the Philadelphia Inquirer points out that while women have been an important part of the craft beer movement in Philadelphia, this is not true for people of color. They cite one of the founders of the first black craft beer festival who suggests that there may only be around 50 black-owned breweries in the United States (Vadala, 2019). So, while black-owned breweries are in the news and there seems to be a buzz of excitement about the industry diversifying, there are still very few black-owned breweries and the two in the Philadelphia area are just in the "getting started" phase of their operation. For comparison, the tourism website, "Visit Philadelphia," boasts that there are more than 90 craft breweries in the Philadelphia area.[2]

## Craft Beer and Gender

The craft beer space is not only a white space, but it is also a male space. In her interesting auto-ethnography, Dunn (2017) talks about how women are not heard within the craft beer space and take up a subordinate position in that space. This happens in several ways. One of the ways that we noticed in our research was the way that tropes of traditional masculinity dominate the space. Men revere strong beers, hoppy beers, dark stouts, and high-gravity beers. The big, bitter, strong beers define a kind of manliness, whereas malty, sweet, fruity beers are seen as somewhat feminine. As Dunn suggests, while these stereotypes are out there, they are also a little more complicated than just presented and further shaped by social class as well.

In general, in the craft beer community, "bigness" is rewarded. The most highly rated beers are usually big beers. Big is a somewhat vague concept but it refers to flavor. A beer that has a lot of hops is a big beer. Further, if it has a lot of hops, then usually the beer has more malt to balance those hops that will tend to push the alcohol content up. But it could also be a strong flavor created by dark malts. It could also be the use of other grains to increase the richness of the mouthfeel. Usually, big beers achieve their bigness by emphasizing one note. They are not subtle or complex beers. And very importantly they are not low-gravity beers, which are often referred to as watery. Bigness is very American and not just something one sees in beer.

And while some women like a big flavored beer, it is a masculine tendency to focus on bigness. As sours became popular, the men in our homebrew group competed to tolerate the sourest flavors and claim they liked them (as they probably did). Learning to like big flavors, high alcohol, extreme sourness, or bitterness is a rite of passage. Darwin (2017) found similar results in her interviews in New York City with craft beer drinkers. There, masculine beer was defined as hoppy, bitter, and high alcohol. Feminine beers, according to her study, were "light, fruity and sweet" (Darwin, 2017, p. 228).

This kind of hierarchical approach to beer tends to support a masculine discourse. It also further defines the space as a masculine space as there is always an inherent competition around big flavors and what is idealized. Other discourses around subtlety and balance are relegated to a subordinate space. It is part of what makes the craft beer bar and craft beer spaces uncomfortable to women. As Dunn suggests in her ethnography, just as we saw with people of color, the space is seen as not a comfortable or welcoming space. And white males, due to white privilege, do not see this and would be confused if someone brought it up to them. This is also not to say that there aren't white males, who prefer subtlety, balance, and lower ABV beers. But their marginalization does not change the nature of the space as a white male space, even when they can be allies for women and men of color.

When we first started to study the craft beer community, we did immediately notice that it was dominantly male (and white as we have said above). But, we were also aware, from the beginning of the research, that more women were drinking beer than you might have seen half a generation ago. So, while all we have said above is very consistent with our research, there did also seem to be a shift as women were slowly finding their place in the craft beer space. And while the masculine psyche was yearning for more big flavors, brewers were interested in creating new and different beers, which meant the space also provided a range of beers, some of which did not fit the "big" criteria and allowed other beer drinkers to find interest in the craft beer bar. Economic and demographic data are beginning to underscore what we were seeing on the ground, and it was not just our ethnographic observations, but there do appear to be new national trends.

In 2018, Bart Watson, chief economist for the Brewers Association drawing on Harris Poll data, said that women made up 31.5% of craft beer drinkers overall (given the way the poll asks the question). While there is an increase in the number of women drinking craft beer over time, the number of craft beer drinkers overall has been going up, so that is not surprising. Watson, then goes on to suggest there are some more important insights from the data. First, since 2015 there has been a 2% shift toward women as they have gone from 29% of the craft beer drinkers in 2015 to 31.5% in 2018. Then by looking at the overall number of craft beer drinkers from 2015 to 2018, in order for women to gain by 2% they need to be just shy of 50% of the new craft beer drinkers in 2018 (Watson, 2018). While two-thirds of the craft beer drinkers are men, the increased number of women has changed the way the beer bar is experienced. Many women know a lot about beer and have strong opinions. They are reviewers of craft beers and fans of particular breweries and brewers. These are not just women following men, but rather they are important consumers and trend setters in the craft beer scene.

When shifting our attention to production, women have worked very hard to gain a foothold in the industry that is still very male dominated. When we began our study, there was a classic gender division of labor in many breweries. The head brewers, assistant brewers, and apprentices tended to be male. And the marketing, branding work was usually women. Marketing reps who went to tap take-overs and beer festivals were sometimes men, but usually women. And teams from a brewery who went to these events often included a male brewer or owner, and a female marketing representative. There have also been husband and wife teams who are co-owners, but often the division of labor is the same, the woman runs the business, the man brews the beer, or started out brewing the beer.

Slowly these things have begun to change. There are a growing number of excellent women brewers in the Philadelphia area and around the world. Part of the change for women in brewing is that apprenticeship opportunities have opened up for more women. Male brewers are taking on more women as apprentices. There are also more opportunities to get formal brewing training through a university program in brewing sciences. As craft beer has become more sophisticated, there is an increasing need for laboratories and lab work maintaining yeast quality and consistency in the brewing process. A number of women scientists have moved into these roles as well including in leadership positions.

Philadelphia has a very active Pink Boots Society chapter and a number of women leaders in the industry. The Pink Boots Society was founded, as they say on their website, to support women and non-binary people in the fermented and alcohol industry. While their definition is broad, they were founded around brewing and particularly the craft beer industry. And they are very active in the craft beer scene. Their founder, Teri Fahrendorf, is a brewer, and the idea was founded during a cross country trip in 2007 where she visited 70 different breweries and participated in the production of a number of beers. During this trip, she realized there were women brewers who did not know about other women who were in a more male-dominated industry. In Philadelphia, Pink Boots sponsors education events, brewing events, and other types of gatherings to support women in craft beer. The founder of the Pink Boots chapter in Philadelphia is the owner of two bar/restaurants and has been on the board of Philly Loves Beer and Philly Beer Week. She has been a dynamic force for women in brewing in the Philadelphia area.

In May of 2021, we had been finished collecting data for a while and we were beginning to write this book, when Brienne Allan, whose Instagram handle is @ratmagnet, posted a question on Instagram asking followers about the sexist comments they experienced. She had had a bad day and was experiencing sexist comments from contractors who were working at the brewery where she worked. The question sparked a huge chain of people sharing their experiences with harassment and sexism. The media began to call this, craft beer's #metoo moment. People were sharing experiences not only around the United States, but women in craft brewing around the world were sharing their experiences. Copenhagen has a particularly creative craft beer scene and one that is connected to the United States through multiple collaborations, and sexual harassment allegations have been made toward a couple of prominent breweries. In Philadelphia, there have been allegations of sexism and harassment leveled at the leadership in a number of important breweries. A case that stood out in the news was about Tired Hands and how the owners have stepped away from day-to-day operations at the brewery. Workers claimed that the management behaved in an unequal and lax way when complaints were made. Several workers suggested there was a toxic male culture that dominated day-to-day operations and Tired Hands main brewpub (Ladd, 2021). The Philly Loves Beer (PLB) board, which hosts the Philly Beer Week, lost two of its board members. One stepped down after allegations of non-consensual sexual activity were leveled at him. The other board member, the above-mentioned founder of the local chapter of the Pink Boots Society, stepped down to protest other board members who were accused of discriminatory activity. Craft beer, which once looked like a progressive industry that was very open and caring toward greater human values, was now looking likc an un-regulated industry where sexism and sexual violence is able to flourish.

## Summary

Craft beer has been caught up in a contradictory development, on the one hand about human liberation, creativity and values go beyond the instrument logic that so dominates our contemporary world (Taylor, 1991). And on the other hand, trapped within the forms of inequality and the racist and sexist practices that have been so much part of the white male world in the United States and elsewhere. We can think of alcoholism, racism, and sexism as the three main malaises of the craft brewing industry. And they are ones that the industry is starting to face. The Brewers Association, the main professional organization of craft brewing, has been taking these issues very seriously in the last few years. In 2018, they named J. Nikol Jackson-Beckham the First Diversity Ambassador at the Brewers Association. Jackson-Beckham has been a craft beer researcher, brewer, and advocate for diversity and inclusion in craft beer across multiple media platforms. They have also paid attention to the gender gap and sexual harassment. There has been perhaps less attention paid to alcoholism in the industry, a tendency that is industry-wide.

As Chapman and Brunsma (2020) pointed out in their book, white supremacy has always been central to the organization of institutions and communities in the United States. And so, racism has been part of beer and brewing too, as these institutions are found within a racist structure. We could make the same comment about sexism and gender inequality. Gender inequality, sexism and misogyny have been a part of American society throughout its history too. So, we should not be surprised that racism and sexism have very much been part of craft beer and its development. As an industry located within a racist and sexist culture, it could not but help reflect some of those distorted values, especially as it did not specifically set out to address these forms of inequality. But it is somewhat ironic that craft beer, an industry that was born from a desire to support craft, creativity and greater equity, should also be trapped in some of society's most basic struggles.

## Notes

1 https://www.brewersassociation.org/insights/shifting-demographics-among-craft-drinkers/
2 https://www.visitphilly.com/articles/philadelphia/essential-craft-breweries-of-greater-philadelphia/

## References

Chapman, N. G., & Brunsma, D. L. (2020). *Beer and racism: How beer became white, why it matters, and the movements to change it.* Bristol: University of Bristol Press.

Darwin, H. (2017). You are what you drink: Gender stereotypes and craft beer preferences within the craft beer scene of New York city. In N. G. Chapman, J. S. Lellock, & C. D. Lippard (Eds.), *Untapped: Exploring the cultural dimensions of craft beer.* Morgantown, WV: West Virginia University Press, 222–235.

Delgaty, A. (2019). The wolf at the door: Human-alcohol collaborations in craft brewing. American Anthropology Association Annual Meeting, Vancouver, BC.

Dunn, J. C. (2017). Does craft beer culture have a place for women? A co-cultural autoethnography. In A. W. Tyma (Ed.), *Beer culture in theory and practice: Understanding craft beer culture in the United States.* Lanham, MD: Lexington Books, pp. 15–33.

Infante, D. (2015). There Are Almost No Black People Brewing Craft Beer. Here's Why. *Thrillist*, March 12. Retrieved from https://www.thrillist.com/drink/nation/there-are-almost-no-black-people-brewing-craft-beer-heres-why

Ladd, J. (2021). At Tired Hands Brewing Company, new leadership hopes to overhaul a 'dude-bro culture'. *The Philadelphia Inquirer*, May 27. Retrieved from https://www.inquirer.com/food/workplace-harassment-restaurants-brewing-tired-hands-20210527.html?utm_medium=referral&utm_source=ios&utm_campaign=app_ios_homefeed_share&utm_content=MUCPDL6STVAMVMA55HEB5KMI5A

Taylor, C. (1991). *The ethics of authenticity.* Boston, MA: Harvard University Press.

Vadala, N. (2019) Diversity in craft beer: 'That whole product and its culture is not even presented to an entire community of people'. *Philadelphia Inquirer.* Retrieved from https://www.inquirer.com/food/drink/diversity-craft-beer-yuengling-homesweet-homebrew-philadelphia-20190503.html#loaded

Watson, B. (2018). Shifting demographics among craft drinkers. *Brewers Association*, June 12. Retrieved from https://www.brewersassociation.org/insights/shifting-demographics-among-craft-drinkers/

Willis, P. (1981). *Learning to labour: How working-class kids get working class jobs* (Morningside ed.). New York, NY: Columbia University Press.

# 9 Conclusion

## Quality over Mass Consumption

The Slow Food movement began in 1986 as a protest against the first McDonald's in Italy opening. The McDonald's in question opened within view of the Spanish Steps in Rome, and the founders of the Slow Food movement found this to be an affront to their national cuisine, architecture, and heritage. They took the greatest umbrage with how McDonald's represented a fast, low-quality food option that disconnected food from heritage, time, and place. Three years later, in their manifesto, they wrote their vision of producing intentionally crafted and slowly produced food.

> Real culture is here to be found. First of all, we can begin by cultivating taste, rather than impoverishing it, by stimulating progress, by encouraging international exchange programs, by endorsing worthwhile projects, by advocating historical food culture and by defending old-fashioned food traditions.[1]

They framed themselves as a rebellion against fast, cultureless food that has no traditions but consumption, and no allegiance but profit. Though countries apart, the craft beer movement in the United States and the Slow Food movement in Italy are cut from the same cloth. These groups privilege the quality of an experience over the ease and cheapness of consuming it. This is an ideological perspective that is at the heart of the craft beer movement, and one that occasionally comes into question as breweries begin to become financially successful or are taken over by "big beer."

It comes as no surprise that the craft beer movement began right around the same time as the Slow Food movement in the 1980s, along with a growing interest in craft and DIY. The massification much of Western society went through in the post-WWII period created a collective ennui among those who sought superior quality or uniqueness in their consumption experiences. Post-WWII consumer society created a homogeneity of experience that by the 1980s had flooded the market with consumption experiences of similar expense and quality. After the original excitement of improving

DOI: 10.4324/9781003109686-9

people's material lives was over, there was a growing demand for something new, something better. The craft beer movement began to coalesce around the desire for better, more interesting beer. But there was also a demand for a greater connection to community, history, and cultural traditions as well as new and innovative tastes and experiences. The Slow Food Movement's manifesto sums up these desires nicely and places them directly at odds with the crushing behemoth of fast food, McDonald's. The emerging craft beer movement of the same time found itself positioned similarly. Adjunct lagers produced by very large breweries that would eventually consolidate into the likes of AB/Inbev and Heineken dominated the market so much so that they were (at least stylistically speaking) the only choice. The craft beer community demanded better flavor and more variety, and since the market was not offering it to them, they decided to do it themselves.

It is this approach that defined the early days of the craft beer movement and that constructed the ideological nucleus of its identity. That identity being one that was centered on the importance of craft, authenticity, quality, and community. These values, of course, needed defining. We discussed these concepts in earlier chapters, and as we noted the ideals of craft are that the brewer cares about all aspects of production, even those that could be overlooked while producing a similar final beer. The attention to detail in every aspect of production is both a by-product of the brewer caring about what they produce, as well as a way of ensuring that what they produce is of high quality and has been done to their standards. The craft is in the adherence to the detailed work of production and also in the creative and imaginative work of adapting and evolving new beer recipes. As the name implies, for craft brewers, the craft component of it is a way of life.

## Community and Authenticity

This idea of craft, and the craft lifestyle, is deeply steeped in the idea of authenticity. Authenticity, though, is a complicated idea. In the eyes of much of the craft-brewing community the authentic brewer is a craft brewer, who owns and controls their brewery, and is brewing on a small scale. But control and production scale are just a small part of the idea of craft authenticity here. More than anything the authentic craft brewer is one who is concerned with the quality of the beer they produce and who also engages in creative and innovative advancement of their beer. An authentic craft brewer, then, is one who understands and adheres to the traditions of brewing and beer style, but also understands these concepts well enough to play and experiment within them to expand them.

But authenticity is not just about the beer produced. It is also about one's place in the community of brewers. Community here is a very important concept. For craft brewers, community conceptually, means to be a good practicing community member, and/or a member in good standing with the arbiters of the craft brewing community. Being a good community member is, of course, evaluated by how one interacts with the various groups the craft brew community considers important to their idea of community. These overlapping, but differentiated, communities are the community of craft brewers (obviously), but also the community of craft beer drinkers and enthusiasts, as well as the community of craft beer bars, pubs, and bottle shops. These communities make different demands of the craft brewer and at times require them to interact with their idea of authenticity in different ways. As discussed in Chapter 7, the communities craft brewers are part of ask them to produce and promote high-quality craft beer, celebrate beer and beer consumption, advance the knowledge of craft beer and its various styles among consumers, and to promote the sale of craft beer. Adhering to all these demands can cause a brewer to be pulled in oppositional directions. For example, the craft beer enthusiast community may want brewers to put on events that showcase new beer styles and that educate them about the nuances of these new styles. The community of craft beer bars may want events more focused on the sale of beer and the celebration of consumption. When brewers are put in positions like this, they are presented with a choice that is emblematic of how the whole craft beer industry functions. The choice, in its most obvious and overt form, is a choice between focusing on producing profit or focusing on adhering to the values of the craft ideology at the possible expense of profit. Certainly, these choices are not mutually exclusive. In fact, both options must be attended to in certain measure for a craft brewery to succeed. But the tension that exists between these choices is one that is ever-present, and one that is used to evaluate a brewer or brewery's adherence to the community standards, and concepts of authenticity and craft itself.

As we have discussed, the central tension is between success being measured as commercial success, and success being measured as adherence to craft principles. The reason for this is not because craft brewers have some innate characteristic that drives them toward producing quality beer, even at the expense of maximizing profit. No. The reason the values in the craft beer community are organized this way is a direct reaction to what the early craft brewers had witnessed from how the big beer business operated. What they saw was a large-scale beer production model that focused on minimizing cost, maximizing profit, extracting as much labor from workers as it could, and ultimately producing what they saw was a bland and underwhelming product. The early craft brewers developed an ideological approach to their craft in response to this. Their ideology was one that rejected the values of big beer (and in many ways the standard values of capitalism). Where big beer sought to maximize profit, cut costs, and produce a product accessible to the widest range of palates, early craft brewers focused their efforts on making the best beer they could, in a way that allowed them to appreciate the experience. To do this, they sought out traditional beer styles that varied from or improved upon those being produced by the big brewers. As they brewed these beers (which they often did for themselves and their friends), they refused to cut corners, refused to adulterate the recipe for the sake of expense, and importantly also refused to work to produce this beer in a way that made their lives less interesting or less pleasurable. Simply, all the approaches big beer had to how it made beer were examined by the craft brewers, who then did the opposite of them. This became the ideology of the craft beer scene. Use the best ingredients, work slowly and purposefully, make the best beer possible, and care about every step in the process.

## Generations

Many of the first generation of craft brewers were not originally entrepreneurs, although there are notable exceptions. Mostly they were hobbyists and craftspeople seeking better beer for themselves and their friends. The beer market being what it was at the time required these people to make their beer themselves. But as they shared their beer, they began to find that there was a demand for it. They began to see that their problem, looking for more interesting beers, was a shared problem with others. They were sharing their beer with friends, in homebrew clubs, and anywhere else they wanted to. Here opinions about the beer, suggestions for improvements to methods or ingredients, and ideas for how the beer could be advanced all were shared. These are the same spaces where the initial demand for their beer came from. "This is great, got any more" or "this is so good I'd pay for it" were likely refrains to them sharing their beer, and before long these early craft brewers began to produce their beer for the market, they became entrepreneurs. As discussed in Chapter 3, generation 0 of the craft beer movement began in the 1970s. But it was still very small, and still mostly focused on home brewing. The year 1971 saw Fritz Maytag's Anchor Brewing produce and bottle its first beer for sale, but this was a very small operation distributing primarily to bars and restaurants in the San Francisco area. A more telling barometer of this time is Charles Papazian's 1976 release of Joy of Brewing. This short text would go on to educate early brewers in how to successfully brew, but also it would encourage them to approach the process slowly, consciously, and with a focus on high-quality end results. It was disseminating what would be established as the craft brewing values as much as it was spreading knowledge of how to brew. It would go on to evolve into *The Complete Joy of Homebrewing*, a sacred text for homebrewers and where many craft brewers first began to educate themselves (Papazian, 1984). The point here is that, while there was increasing interest in craft beer, the market for it in the first generation was very small and just developing. Craft beer then was necessarily a labor of love.

This remained true through the first generation of craft brewers. While the market made small steps toward being more stable for them, the real shift here is in the number of existing craft breweries. More than anything, this first generation solidified the values of the craft beer community. This happened as a persistent act of resistance to what big beer was, but more than that it happened out of necessity. In these early days, knowledges were incomplete, access to resources differed by brewer, equipment was less-than-perfect, and most breweries were just keeping their heads above water financially. This meant that sharing between craft breweries (supplies, knowledge, equipment, and even labor) was necessary for their success and for the success of the craft beer scene. To borrow a tired phrase, the rising tide of interest in craft beer raised the boats of all craft breweries. Certainly, some breweries did better financially as the market for craft beer grew, but the culture of working together and sharing to allow for the best products to be produced, while still competing in the marketplace, was firmly established by the end of the first generation. The most often told story about the enduring nature of these craft values is how Jim Koch of Boston Beer Company, who was often at odds with the community of craft brewers and seen as an outsider, opened the brewery's hops reserve during the 2008 unprecedented hops shortage and shared his supply with other craft brewers. He shared hundreds of pounds of hops with craft breweries, asking only that they pay what the hops had cost his brewery. This allowed Koch to share hops during a massive shortage to craft brewers at a price sometimes $25 cheaper a pound than they could be found on the open market.[2] At a time when profit-seeking could have been easily done, the craft values guided Koch to prop up the craft beer community instead of exploiting his position within it.

By the second generation (roughly 1994–2000), craft beer had firmly established a position within the beer market. It had officially moved from being a collection of passion projects into a successful industry. In the first year of the second generation of craft brewing, there was a 50% increase in breweries in the United States. Money was flowing into the scene, brewers were experiencing real financial success for the first time, and the craft beer market began to feel stable. Breweries began to expand in all directions. They expanded the size of their breweries to expand production, as such they also expanded their distribution and market share. They also began to experiment with their recipes to evolve them and expand their range of beer offerings. This generation developed new beer styles that are still incredibly popular (the American style IPA is a good example), but to grow as they did many had to become businesses unlike those they had previously been. Expansion required loans, investors, or shareholders. They demanded repayment and/or return on investment, which meant that craft brewers who had expanded in this way now had a required focus on profit. Profit had always been a driver, but it was becoming indispensable. It is for these indebted breweries where the first real challenges to the craft value system would come into play. Reducing production costs to increase profit, while forsaking some aspects of quality, was absolutely a way that some breweries in difficult positions decided to go. But at the time the craft industry was booming, most breweries were not having any trouble maintaining their quality while also repaying their loans or paying out their investors. These tensions that would be more powerful in the coming years were emerging though. The chips in the craft beer mug were beginning to show.

The early days of the third generation of craft beer seemingly had everything going for them. There was increasing public interest in craft beer, investors and loans were easy to come by, and more and more people (well, largely middle-class white men) who were successful homebrewers were turning to try their hand at making a living at it, even the craft beer consuming market was expanding both in how much of the overall market they were and in the styles of beer they were willing to try. Success was abundant for many breweries, but so was the potential to damage their brand and reputation by being perceived as "selling out." For craft breweries, "selling out" would be doing something (or appearing to do something) that violated their adherence to craft values, most obviously this is the pursuit of profit over the pursuit of quality and innovation. For the third generation of breweries, identity politics was becoming something that they all needed to be concerned with. It was the height of the craft ideology where values of authenticity, community, taste experience, and craft were more important than profit. It was a community creating a new kind of economy with a different set of values.

## Digital Media

Digital and social media became a major component (sometimes the only component) of how many craft breweries marketed themselves and announced new products. But it also became the place where people went to get a sense of who a brewery was socially, culturally, and ideologically. It was the space where they built their reputation and developed their identity. As we've noted, these identities needed to be maintained as the brewery cultivated a following and tried to become successful. But with success, or the attempt at it, a brewery could be perceived as selling out, or violating their craft ideals. With social media this all played out in something like real time and allowed anyone who wanted to weigh in on what they thought of a brewery, their beer, or how they were operating. The potential to lose face or lose the control of their narrative was high. It certainly wasn't all bad though.

Digital media such as the internet and discussion lists helped the early craft brewers share knowledge, buy equipment, collaborate, and cultivate a market on their websites. The rise of social media was incredibly advantageous for small breweries. Free marketing and event promotion was a godsend for them. Many small craft breweries were operating on shoestring budgets. Sure, this was a boom-time for craft breweries, but new ones were popping up all over. By 2010, the craft beer market had really taken off, as had the sheer number of craft breweries around. There were just shy of 2000 craft breweries in the United States in 2010. The market had shown slow, but steady growth (there were about 1500 craft breweries in 2000). In the coming decade, the market would explode, and the number of craft breweries would more than triple (9247 as of 2021).[3] The rapid increase at this time was not fueled by social media or increased market interest alone though. Third generation brewers had an advantage that no other generation had. This was that they could buy used high-quality, large-scale commercial brewing equipment at a fraction of the cost that it would cost new. It was available from other breweries that collapsed, or ones that were upgrading their system. This meant that third generation craft brewers had the best market to work in, the easiest time promoting themselves, the best equipment available to them at low cost, as well as the best ingredients. It was a good time to get into the game.

The early days of the third generation were very idealistic. Brewers generally cooperated, shared knowledge and resources when they could, and did their best to work together to make the craft beer scene work for everyone. The oft-told story that exemplifies this era is the "collaboration not litigation" beer that Russian River and Avery breweries co-produced. In 2004, without knowledge that the other was doing it, both breweries had been selling a beer called Salvation. When the breweries became aware of this, instead of filing copyright claims and injunctions the two breweries worked together to produce the "Collaboration, Not Litigation Ale," which was a blend of the two different Salvation beers. By 2006, it was for sale and the craft beer community had this feel-good story to roll out if the values of the craft beer industry came into question or when they needed an example of craft beer's pro-social ideals.

## Current Tensions

But boom-time success breeds competition, and competition can erode some of the values that the craft brewing community held so dear. Craft beer grew quickly as a business through the 2010s, but this also meant the market for it started to get saturated. Further, the craft market was not exclusively occupied by craft brewers anymore. Big brewing conglomerates (e.g., AB InBev and Sapporo) were working their way into the scene. The most famous example here is Chicago-based craft brewery Goose Island. They are one of the go-to stories of selling out in the craft beer scene. When Goose Island's owner, Greg Hall, decided to step away from the business, AB Inbev stepped in and bought the brewery for $38.8M (Hall et al. got $22.5M for 58% and the Craft Brewers Alliance got $16.3M for their 42%). AB InBev kept the name and the beers and expanded production and distribution. The feeling in the craft community was that InBev was masquerading as a craft beer, trying to gain a foothold in the craft scene and disrupt the now-profitable market. But the community would not be duped. Cries of "sell-out!" rang out throughout it, and Goose Island was deemed faux craft at best. On the other hand, in 2019 New Belgium sold to Lion Little World Beverages, an Australian subsidiary of the Japanese giant Kirin. And that merger is seen as a hopeful success story for maintaining quality and craft ideals.

These stories are important because they illustrates a point where craft brewers began to be skeptical of each other, of investors, and of how their competitors were behaving behind closed doors. "How much money, and whose, was really getting pumped into these breweries" was becoming an increasing, and paranoia-inducing thought that many craft brewers were experiencing. The effect of this is that those craft values that shaped the industry early on were becoming harder to adhere to. Sure, craft brewers will still tell you how important dedication to quality is, how valuable knowledge-sharing and collaboration are, how important it is to maintain the spirit of community in the craft scene, and how important living by the craft ideology is. But these days it comes with caveats. The act of practicing craft ideals is now plagued by the idea that other breweries are behaving like bad actors to increase their profit and market share, or perhaps more simply, that others' outward credibility masks some profit-first motivations. This idea is pervasive, because to some extent it is now true of all craft breweries. They all must care about the bottom-line, and generating profit is at least as much of a concern as producing high-quality products. The craft beer market got big and saturated, and the internal contradictions between craft ideals and profit came home to roost.

The craft brewing scene of today seems to be one where brewers adhere to craft values with those they know they can trust to also do so, but with others the approach is litigation, not collaboration (Thornley, 2017). The days of share and share alike are gone. They are remembered fondly but thought to be outdated and ill-suited for how the craft market operates today. They are a quaint idea from a simpler time, that are good to adhere to in theory, but can be problematic in practice. Craft breweries of today are undeniably businesses, and they are no longer ashamed of this moniker. The craft values are still alive, and they do still influence the way that many brewers and breweries operate, but for a craft brewery to survive today they must keep their balance sheet in the black, and have profit be an important factor in all their business decision-making.

As the craft community became aware of this collective shift away from what were the traditional ideals and values, they also came to view the entire industry with an increased degree of criticality. This is not to say that the idea of the craft-dedicated, friendly, pro-social brewer was destroyed. It was more reflected on with the idea that it needed to be amended.

The early craft beer pioneers built the idea that to be a successful craft brewer the majority of what one needed was a dedication to craft, a willingness to learn, an understanding of beer and its traditions, a hard-working nature, and a willingness to persevere through tough or lean times. While those in the industry and some homebrewers would recognize this as a mythologized caricature of craft beer, much of the consuming public latched onto this image as another reason to buy this superior beer. But as the market saturated in the third generation, the veneer began to rub off this image. This happened largely because the public began to become aware that the craft beer scene, but more specifically craft brewing, was not as open to everyone as they had once believed. The many barriers to entry were becoming more apparent.

The sheer cost of brewing, even as a hobby, is one big barrier. Dedicated home brewers have long been aware that home brewing is not a cheap or easy hobby. Ingredients are expensive, a certain amount of space is required to brew and then ferment the beer, the process requires precision and exemplary cleanliness, and even when closely watched the whole process can go frustratingly wrong (mostly in terms of a spoiled batch, but also in terms of spills, mistimed pitches, scorched malt, etc.). As interest in craft beer grew and more people tried their hand at home brewing, they learned this as well. And so, while the idea of the brewer remained one of the dedicated craftsmen diligently working with care to produce a quality product, it also shifted to include the knowledge that these were largely middle-class white men who romanticized the practice and ideals of craft beer while also fetishizing the labor involved in doing it, associating it with the idea that it connects them to long gone generations of mythologized bucolic brewers. This is most present in small-scale brewers and home brewers, but even the big craft breweries are crowded with people who started out small and grew up. This image of the hard-working brewer is still with them, and it can be a tough image to overcome as well as a problematic one. Tough because it is so intertwined with what craft beer views as its values, and problematic because when many brewers actually conjure this image it appears to them as a middle-class straight white man. This has an impact on what spaces individuals who do not fit this model are allowed to access in the industry and what ones they are gatekept away from.

As we have said, this means that the traditional model is the men do the brewing and the women handle the marketing and sales. There are, of course, forms of misogyny, racism, sexism, and homophobia embedded in this. For much of craft beer's history, these issues simmered under the surface. But now, in 2022, they are bubbling up and being reckoned with. The issues were obvious in hindsight, those that did not fit the idealized model of the brewer, or those that wished to step out of a traditional role, were met with harassment, dismissal, or other unfair treatment. Certainly, this is not true of every brewery or every interaction, but it has been reported frequently enough across the industry that it is now considered an industry-wide issue to be dealt with. As the saying goes, acceptance is the first step to recovery. And it would seem that the industry has accepted that there is an issue. Whether it will recover from these issues, and the reputational damage some breweries have suffered from having committed them, is yet to be seen. Certainly, the hope is that craft beer becomes more inclusive, more accepting, and more reflective in how it operates from here on out. Obviously, it will be good for those who have suffered due to the harassment, ridicule, and resistance they have met. It will also be good for craft beer as a culture and product.

Where does that leave the state of the culture and the industry? Well, craft beer does still represent a resistance to big beer. It still represents an ideology of favoring craft and quality and process over efficiency and low-cost production for profit, even if this is not always the practice of some of the now very big breweries in the craft scene. It is still a place for creative, innovative, and forward-thinking brewers to work to push the boundaries of craft beer to evolve. And, even with its issues, it is still an inclusive place for people who reject fast, cheap low-quality beer in favor of slower, more expensive, better beer. But, as described, it is still largely the preserve of the middle class (the expense alone either as producer or consumer ensures this). It is still also overwhelmingly white and male and overtly heterosexual. There are brewers and breweries that are exceptions to this trend (The Queer Brewing Project comes to mind here), but by and large the whole of the culture is white, male, heterosexual, and middle-class.

What does the future hold for craft beer then? This is hard to say. The trends seem to indicate that there will continue to be consolidation of large craft breweries to increase market share, as well as the persistent issues that come with the need for big money investors who can facilitate expansion. It also seems that big beer will continue to work their way into the market, creating brands that masquerade as craft beers or buying controlling interest in ones that are willing to sell (just this month Sapporo bought Stone Brewing for $165 million).[4] But the craft beer community seems as strong as ever, and they are still passionate about craft. Simply, they still care about the values that craft has always purported, and they are still able to tell the difference between craft beer and faux-craft beer as well as why that matters to them. And there are many smaller craft breweries and brewpubs that are independent and do not draw as much interest from big investors. Hopefully, craft beer culture will work to be more inclusive, and will contend with its past and present failings. The early signs are that it is working in this direction, though with some resistance from the conservative traditionalists. Perhaps this ideology will age out along with the dinosaurs who think it. But this is unlikely. Inclusion requires a demand for it, and hopefully those who have made the issues in the craft scene public will continue to demand inclusion and acceptance for those who historically have not had it.

## Final Thoughts

With all the issues and problems we have discussed, for us, craft beer still represents a place of great resistance to the profit-first capitalist ideology that dictates so many other arenas of consumption. It is still a place where values, quality, a respect for tradition and history, and a demand for creative evolution are all critically important. For the craft beer community, these things are as important as how good the beer is. Further, the utopian moment of craft beer has been a very interesting experiment in the creation of an economy where the activities that are most valued are largely pro-social. The thing that drives major capitalists is making money. Aglietta (2016, p. 27) points out that most modern economic theory excludes money from the theory. And that is because it does not fit into their model of a system seeking equivalence. But money is the very thing that drives the economic system and the thing that drives the participants in that system. What Graeber (2001) has shown us is that this is a social activity (or game) like Kula, where the society admires the powerful players of the game. And the players and the objects created in their play become highly valuable (in the economic sense) because we all think this is the most important activity. But making the most money, and accumulating the most profit, is destroying the planet. And really, there is no need for this. What we can see, in this brief moment, in the small community of craft beer, is that highly valued activity, and high-status people and products do not need to be destructive to the environment or the communities people live in. It is a small model (and there have been other examples too) of an economy that can be fun and challenging for the producers and consumers and be good for all in the process.

## Notes

1 https://slowfood.com/filemanager/Convivium%20Leader%20Area/Manifesto_ENG.pdf
2 https://www.supermarketnews.com/center-store/sam-adams-shares-its-hops
3 https://www.brewersassociation.org/statistics-and-data/national-beer-stats/
4 https://www.thedrinksbusiness.com/2022/06/japanese-brewery-sapporo-acquires-stone-brewing-for-165-million/

## References

Aglietta, M. (2016). *Money: 5000 years of debt and power*. New York, NY: Verso.

Graeber, D. (2001). *Toward an anthropological theory of value: The false coin of our own dreams*. New York, NY: Palgrave Macmillan.

Papazian, C. (1984). *The complete joy of homebrewing*. New York, NY: Avon Books.

Thornley, D. (2017). Litigation, not collaboration: The changing landscape of trademark disputes in the craft-beer industry. *Marquette Intellectual Property Law Review*, 21. Available from https://scholarship.law.marquette.edu/iplr/vol21/iss2/6

# Index

Note: Page numbers in *italics* refer to figures.

www.ingramcontent.com/pod-product-compliance
Ingram Content Group UK Ltd.
Pitfield, Milton Keynes, MK11 3LW, UK
UKHW020137200926
475702UK00005B/788
* 9 7 8 0 3 6 7 6 2 5 5 9 7 *